Economic

# FAS
# CHANGING
# WORLD

## Making The Complex Simple

**PHIL RUTHVEN**

WP

Published by:
Wilkinson Publishing Pty Ltd
ACN 006 042 173
Level 4, 2 Collins St Melbourne, Victoria, Australia 3000
Ph: +61 3 9654 5446
www.wilkinsonpublishing.com.au

National Library of Australia Cataloguing-in-Publication entry:
Creator:    Ruthven, Phillip K., author
Title:      Fast-changing world / Phil Ruthven.
ISBN:       9781925642056 (paperback)
Subjects:   Economic forecasting--Australia.
            Social prediction--Australia.
            Knowledge management--Australia.
            Change.
            Common fallacies.

Printed in Australia

Phil Ruthven is the founder of IBISWorld, an international corporation providing online business information, forecasting and strategic services. IBISWorld now operates in Australia, the United States (NY and LA), Canada, China, the United Kingdom and Indonesia. It plans to add the rest of the European Union, and Japan over the next five years or so. In 2014, Phil became a Member of the Order of Australia in recognition of his significant service to business and commerce, and to the community.

Phil contributes regularly to radio, TV, newspapers, magazines and documentaries on business, economic and social issues. He continues to be one of Australia's most frequent and prolific commentators in demand by the media, and is widely considered the nation's most respected strategist and futurist on business, social and economic matters.

He addresses about 40-50 congresses, seminars and conferences each year and has done so for three decades. His involvement as a communicator takes him around Australia and occasionally overseas.

Phil is a science graduate with further studies in management and economics at various universities and institutes, and was a Rotary awardee to the United States in the late 1960s. He spent over 10 years in the food industry, including executive positions in research, production and marketing, before establishing IBIS (later renamed IBISWorld) in 1971.

Phil is currently an Adjunct Professor at The University of Technology (Sydney), and a member of the ANU College of Business & Economics Advisory Board.  He is a recent past board member of the Melbourne Institute and CEDA, and a past Director of Open Family Australia (the charitable foundation aiding street children), where he continues to help as an Ambassador for Whitelion/Open Family.

IBISWorld has earned the reputation as an astute forecasting and advisory corporation, based on its unique and comprehensive databases. Its website www.ibisworld.com.au is rated as one of the most sophisticated and powerful industry and marketing websites in the world today. Its foresight and insight of business trends is outstanding, with the most envious record of accuracy among its peers. Their clients include over 1600 of Australia's large corporations and government authorities, and over 5000 major US corporate and institutional clients. IBISWorld has become the premier provider of industry information in the United States, Canada, Australia, China, the United Kingdom, Germany, New Zealand and other nations. It also produces global industry reports on selected industries and markets.

It is a privately owned company employing over 450 staff, growing at 15-20% per annum in revenue.

# Contents

# Foreword

We are virtually swamped with information these days, and it is impossible to keep up with it all. It is hard enough to keep up to date in our own job, given all the new ideas, technologies and this digital-disruption era that everybody talks about. Let alone all the other stuff.

They say all the world's knowledge accumulated over the past several thousand years doubles every two-and-a-half years. Yikes. It gets worse. How do we know what is true and what is false? What is hearsay, exaggerations, scuttlebutt, mistruths and outright lies, versus evidence-based facts and truths?

Facts usually ruin a good story, as they say. And that is what I have been doing for nearly half a century; hopefully making truths just as interesting as the untruths in speeches and writings.

But more than that, it is important to get perspective these days; what some people call a helicopter view. We choose, or are forced into, narrow areas of interest: in our work, recreation and other pursuits. And we are forced into short-termism rather than the long-term view.

It is truly alarming how little our political leaders know about the things that matter and what the future could be, whether it is where industries of the future are, where the jobs are, or where the world is going. This leads to the scaremongers having a field day: robots will take over most of our jobs; marriages don't last as long as they used to; the murder rate is rising to record levels; the rich are getting richer in Australia, and the poor are getting poorer; ageing will mean we will run out of workers; foreigners will soon own most of Australia; and on they go. None of the above is true.

The reality is that things are generally getting better. Our standard of living – the goods and services we can buy today – is seven times higher than a century ago, and is approaching four times higher than at the end of the Industrial Age, as far back as 1965. Yes, four times.

Why worry about our Manufacturing industry now being only 6% of our economy and 7% of our jobs, compared with 29% or more for both 50 years ago, when our standard of living has risen – not fallen – that much? Agriculture was once 50% of the economy and all the jobs; it now contributes just over 2% to the economy and less than 3% of all jobs, and the sky hasn't fallen in, Chicken Little!

And then we hear that the only wealth-creating jobs are where you make things, so we should go back to manufacturing, even though the wages there have fallen well below the national average of all 12 million jobs in the country. No: most manufacturing now belongs to developing economies, not the advanced ones like ours. It really is scary where these silly ideas come from.

The fact is, the best is yet to come. And hopefully, the facts, realities and trends outlined in these short articles will surprise you, get you thinking, and make you happier, more confident and positive about where we are and the unfolding future: for us, our children and unborn generations to come.

Phillip Ruthven AM
Futurist • Strategist • Forecaster

Yes, it is true: housing is expensive in Australia. Measured as a multiple of average wages, Sydney housing is nearly one-and-a-half times that of London, and over twice that of New York. All of Australia's eight capital cities are dearer than Boston, Washington, Chicago and Tokyo. Shortly, we will look at whether we are facing a serious shake-out in prices, and if affordability is on a knife edge or not.

But first, some top-down statistics, as shown in the chart below.

**The housing market at a glance**
June 2017 (E)

- **Population**        24.5 million
- **Dwellings**        10.3 million (9.6 million occupied)
- **Type**        Houses/flats et al. (74/26)
- **Value**        $6.55 trillion
  **New Finance**        $393 billion in F2017
  **Mortgage Debt**        $2.2 trillion
- **Average Price**        Dwellings $636,000
- **Affordability**        Dwelling price 4.0 times average household income
- **Median Price**
  (Eight Capital Cities)

| | |
|---|---|
| Dwellings | $715,000 |
| Houses | $785,000 |
| Flats et al. | $560,000 |

SOURCE: IBISWORLD 01/04/17

We are expected to have over 10 million dwellings valued at over $6.5 trillion in F2017 — almost four times the nation's annual gross domestic product (GDP) — with almost three times as many houses as we have flats and apartments. The average dwelling price totals just over four times the average household income, and is estimated to have a value of $636,000 in June this year.

Our population density equates to just over 2.5 people per dwelling: twice that at the beginning of the last century in 1901. Our dwellings are now much bigger – they have almost tripled in size – with dwellings of three bedrooms or more accounting for almost three-quarters of all dwellings.

Australians will have borrowed almost $400 billion this fiscal year on new housing plus alterations and additions to existing dwellings, as the next chart shows.

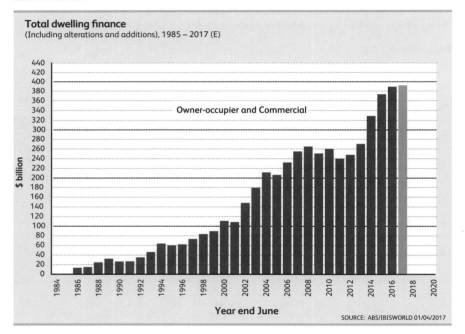

**Total dwelling finance**
(Including alterations and additions), 1985 – 2017 (E)

Owner-occupier and Commercial

Year end June

SOURCE: ABS/IBISWORLD 01/04/2017

We can afford all this on top of existing debt, as the two charts on the next page suggest.

Debt servicing at 8.6% of disposable income is close to the average of the past 40 years (8.0%), which can be attributed to record-low interest rates.

## Our Capital Cities

Excluding city-states such as Singapore and Hong Kong, Australia's population is

## Household debt servicing ratio
% of household disposable income, to F2016

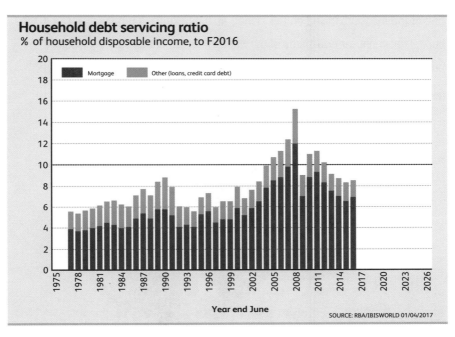

SOURCE: RBA/IBISWORLD 01/04/2017

## Indicator lending rates
Australia F1960–2016

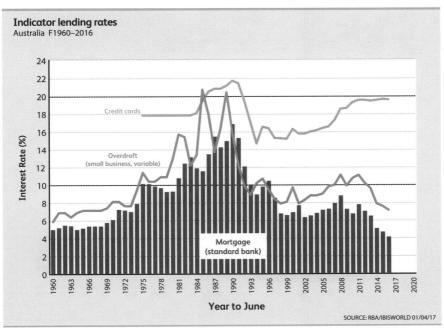

SOURCE: RBA/IBISWORLD 01/04/17

one of the most urbanised on the planet, as the next chart reminds us. Our eight capitals account for two-thirds of our population, yet prices vary enormously between these cities, as the second chart below shows so starkly.

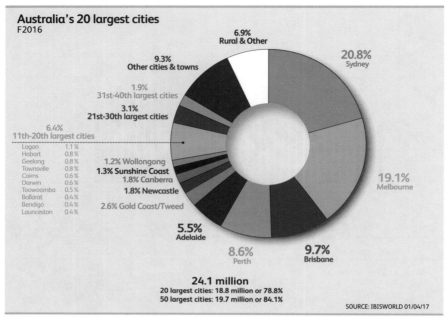

**Australia's 20 largest cities**
F2016

6.9%
Rural & Other

20.8%
Sydney

9.3%
Other cities & towns

1.9%
31st-40th largest cities

3.1%
21st-30th largest cities

6.4%
11th-20th largest cities

| | |
|---|---|
| Logan | 1.1% |
| Hobart | 0.8% |
| Geelong | 0.8% |
| Townsville | 0.8% |
| Cairns | 0.6% |
| Darwin | 0.6% |
| Toowoomba | 0.5% |
| Ballarat | 0.4% |
| Bendigo | 0.4% |
| Launceston | 0.4% |

1.2% Wollongong
**1.3% Sunshine Coast**
1.8% Canberra
**1.8% Newcastle**
2.6% Gold Coast/Tweed

19.1%
Melbourne

5.5%
Adelaide

8.6%
Perth

9.7%
Brisbane

**24.1 million**
20 largest cities: 18.8 million or 78.8%
50 largest cities: 19.7 million or 84.1%

SOURCE: IBISWORLD 01/04/17

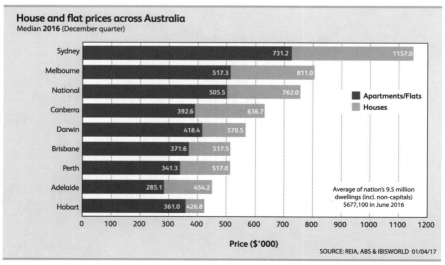

**House and flat prices across Australia**
Median **2016** (December quarter)

| | Apartments/Flats | Houses |
|---|---|---|
| Sydney | 731.2 | 1157.0 |
| Melbourne | 517.3 | 811.0 |
| National | 505.5 | 762.0 |
| Canberra | 392.6 | 636.7 |
| Darwin | 418.4 | 570.5 |
| Brisbane | 371.6 | 517.5 |
| Perth | 341.3 | 517.0 |
| Adelaide | 285.1 | 454.2 |
| Hobart | 361.0 | 426.8 |

■ Apartments/Flats
■ Houses

Average of nation's 9.5 million
dwellings (incl. non-capitals)
$677,100 in June 2016

**Price ($'000)**

SOURCE: REIA, ABS & IBISWORLD 01/04/17

Sydney is the odd one out, given its prices are so far ahead of the second priciest, Melbourne. The next two charts suggest the degree to which Sydney and Melbourne prices seem to be well above trend. Both are in 'bubble territory' – Sydney alarmingly so.

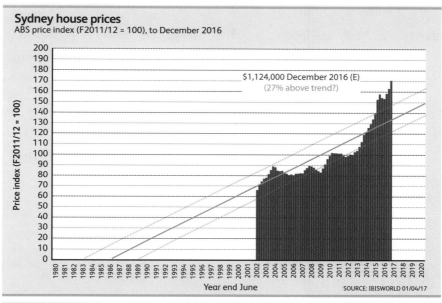

### Sydney house prices
ABS price index (F2011/12 = 100), to December 2016

$1,124,000 December 2016 (E)
(27% above trend?)

Price index (F2011/12 = 100)

Year end June

SOURCE: IBISWORLD 01/04/17

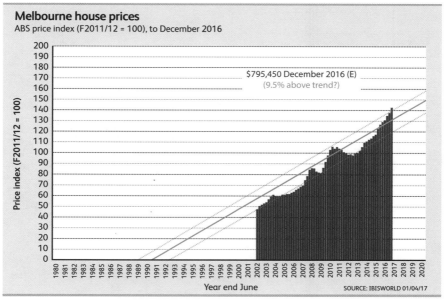

### Melbourne house prices
ABS price index (F2011/12 = 100), to December 2016

$795,450 December 2016 (E)
(9.5% above trend?)

Price index (F2011/12 = 100)

Year end June

SOURCE: IBISWORLD 01/04/17

In December 2016, Sydney house prices were thought to be 27% above trend, while Melbourne house prices were estimated at a more modest 9.5% above trend.

The difference is even more marked when just apartments and flats are compared between the two big cities. Sydney's apartments are also in 'bubble territory', in contrast to Melbourne's below-trend performance due to oversupply (especially in the city's CBD).

As observed in the following two charts, Sydney was undersupplied for nearly a decade leading up to 2013; and its apartment prices in December 2016 were thought to be 18% above trend. In contrast, Melbourne went into overdrive during this period, resulting in a buyers' market with apartment prices below trend by some 5%.

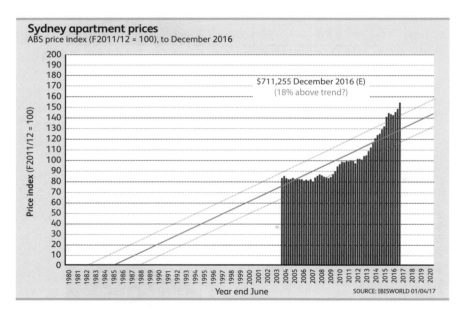

**Sydney apartment prices**
ABS price index (F2011/12 = 100), to December 2016

$711,255 December 2016 (E)
(18% above trend?)

Price index (F2011/12 = 100)

Year end June

SOURCE: IBISWORLD 01/04/17

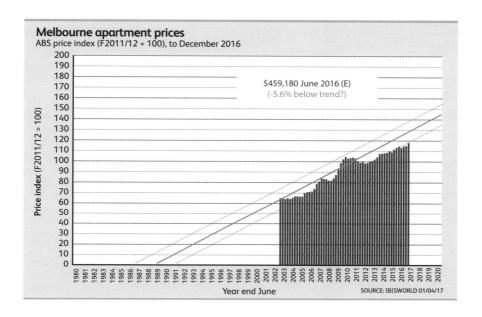

**Melbourne apartment prices**
ABS price index (F2011/12 = 100), to December 2016

$459,180 June 2016 (E)
(-5.6% below trend?)

Price index (F2011/12 = 100)

Year end June

SOURCE: IBISWORLD 01/04/17

Indications are that price growth is now abating as we head into 2017; and some capital cities are seeing falling prices. So, what does this mean?

Firstly, Australia's economy is not threatened by its world-leading dwelling prices: they are affordable according to the earlier debt servicing chart (page 3), where the ratio is the lowest in some five decades. The chart on the next page reinforces the fact that we have lived with an affordability ratio in the high range (three-and-a-half to four times the value of household incomes) for a decade and a half, without dire things happening.

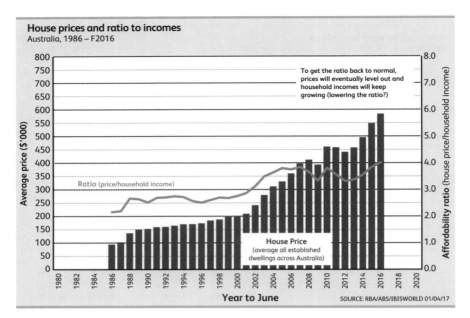

**House prices and ratio to incomes**
Australia, 1986 – F2016

To get the ratio back to normal, prices will eventually level out and household incomes will keep growing (lowering the ratio?)

Ratio (price/household income)

House Price
(average all established dwellings across Australia)

Year to June

SOURCE: RBA/ABS/IBISWORLD 01/04/17

Average price ($'000)

Affordability ratio (house price/household income)

Yes, Australia's household debt (mainly mortgage debt) as a share of GDP is one of the highest in the world; but it is manageable. And our corporate debt and government debt as a share of GDP are among the lowest, if not actually the lowest, in the world. Overall, we are not living too far above our means compared with most other developed nations.

Sydney is the stand-out loner among our capital cities in regards to housing affordability, with Melbourne not that far behind (especially with houses). NSW's economy is doing well – indeed, it is the best in the nation – but that may not protect it from a dwelling price correction in the year or so ahead, or a longish period of flatlining in prices until incomes catch up to restore equanimity. Melbourne is not doing so well, with a higher unemployment rate; and the housing market is probably more vulnerable.

So, while there is room for concern in our two biggest cities, it is not panic stations for the nation at large. But we do need to increase supply; and we do need to warn homebuyers of the dangers of going too deep into debt when interest rates are rising.

# Robots, the Digital Era and Jobs

*Company Director* magazine April 2017

Just how much should we worry – or even panic – about where artificial intelligence (AI), cognitive learning systems, big data, very high-speed broadband, analytics, robots and general automation are taking us? Even those words can be scary, with or without us being completely au fait with their meaning.

Will we automate so many jobs that we end up with a divided and divisive labour force and a society with frightening unemployment? Will robots be smarter than us and be able to reproduce themselves as Bill Gates predicted? Is science fiction becoming reality?

In the debate about running out of workers (the ageing population) or running out of jobs (automation and robots), it is useful to begin with the proportion of the population that want a job. This is termed the labour force (see chart next page), the workforce being those that have jobs, and the difference being the unemployed.

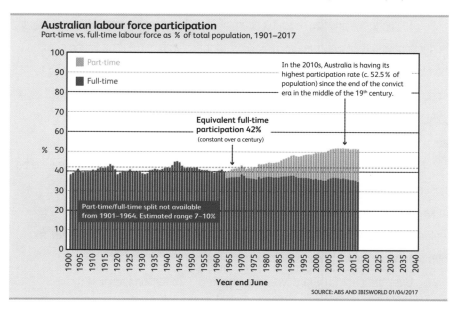

**Australian labour force participation**
Part-time vs. full-time labour force as % of total population, 1901–2017

Part-time
Full-time

In the 2010s, Australia is having its highest participation rate (c. 52.5 % of population) since the end of the convict era in the middle of the 19th century.

**Equivalent full-time participation 42%**
(constant over a century)

Part-time/full-time split not available from 1901–1964. Estimated range 7–10%

Year end June

SOURCE: ABS AND IBISWORLD 01/04/2017

Barely 40% of the population put their hand up for work in 1900. Today that figure exceeds 52%, with more than 49% of that 52% getting jobs. The average working week (annualised) for the nation's 12 million workers is around 30 hours after allowing for annual leave, public holidays, sick leave and long-service leave. All up, this amounts to two months off each year.

## Employment evolution

In the early 19th century, a full-time job was a week of 65 hours without the benefits listed above. We now work less than half those hours each year, but for a duration of 50 years instead of 25 years, because we live over twice as long as our forebears did. So, today's so-called 'full-time' jobs are part-time by historical standards.

One of the big changes in the new age of service industries and information and communications technology (ICT) of the past half-century, has been the rise in part-time and casual employment, which we now define in terms of being less than 15 hours per week. In 2017, part-time and casual employment accounts for 34% of the labour force, one of the highest in the world.

To suggest a position requiring hours of 15 or less is not a proper job is to insult students paying their way through university, mothers with babies and young children, the elderly wanting the dignity of work but with fewer hours, the injured returning to work, and the disabled and mentally-limited. The progressive reduction in hours of work points to one of the reasons we have never run out of jobs despite labour-saving or labour-displacement technology: we share the available work around.

By the end of this century we could expect the average working week to be closer to 24-25 hours – again on an annualised basis.

To say new technologies means losing jobs overlooks the ones we create to replace them. Over the past five years, we have created almost seven times more jobs than we have lost. Yes, seven times more.

Over the past 50 years, we have created 3.25 million jobs just by outsourcing household activities and chores. These account for more than a third of today's 12 million jobs. And we have created more through new exports and through business functions outsourcing. New pervasive technology such as ICT employs 350,000 people; and this utility is now into the second stage of its evolution (as of 2007) with a digital era of fast broadband, big data, analytics and cognitive-learning programming (a newer term for artificial intelligence, or AI).

Technology has both created and removed jobs throughout history. In the early 1820s, agriculture employed half the nation's workforce; now it accounts for just 2.5%. Tractors, tilling and harvesting equipment, fertiliser and genetic modification forced that reduction. Manufacturing once employed 29% of the workforce; now, six decades later, it accounts for just 8%. Machines, just-in-time manufacturing, outsourced non-core functions, consumer saturation and imports all contributed to the decline.

## Where are we heading?

Currently, the largest employing industry is health and community services at 1.6 million, followed by retailing at 1.2 million. Health numbers are likely to go up for many decades to come, but retail – or at least its share of total employment – is expected to decline with the online shopping revolution underway.

All this begs the question: what systems and technology changes are threatening jobs in 2017 and beyond? The primary and secondary sectors – with barely 20% of all jobs these days – are largely automated, and may shrink to 15-16% of the labour force by the middle of this 21$^{st}$ century.

It is the services sectors and their industries which make up four-fifths of jobs that are more under threat from robots and digital disruption. The tertiary services sector of wholesaling, retailing and transport is likely to shrink a bit through automation and online shopping; perhaps down to 14-15% of all jobs from its current 18%.

The quinary sector of hospitality, health, arts, sport and recreation, and other personal services will grow, more aided by technology rather than threatened by it. Already accounting for 26% of all jobs, its growth could actually soak up the lost share from the previously mentioned sectors. Or nearly.

It may well be the only other sector, the quaternary sector, that is most threatened by robots and the digital era. Finance, legal services, accounting services, consulting, tertiary education, many government services, and administrative and support services are all in the firing line. These, and others in the quaternary sector, account for more than a third of all jobs in 2017. AI programs are already cutting into many professional services such as legal, tax advice, auditing and a wide range of consulting services.

And what about robots? As long as we don't envisage them only as humanoids such as C-3PO and R2D2 from *Star Wars*, they are already everywhere for individuals and households in the form of heart pacemakers, cochlear hearing devices, soon-to-come sight-bionics, DSC skid controlling, and crash avoidance technology. Thousands more like this are on the way, for both households and workers.

But are robots smarter than humans? Of course: it is already true. We see computers winning chess championships and quiz programs. As Abraham Lincoln once reputably said, 'God must so love the common man, he created so many of them'. So, leaders and good governments must accept the challenge to educate and protect individuals and encourage their self-esteem.

We do not need scaremongering, sincere but amateur fantasists, nor sitting-on-one's-hands. The future is far more prospective than to do anything other than embrace it, but with some safeguards. Above all, we must remember that job-sharing by ever-falling hours of annual work is just as important as planning for totally new jobs in maintaining a fully-employed society.

The September 2015 newsletter set out to create perspective for Australia's place in the Asia Pacific region for the 21st century. In this newsletter, we revisit this issue and broaden our scope to Greater Asia (including the Indian subcontinent). The proposed departure (Brexit) of the UK from the EU and the latter's potential for other difficulties and defections, coupled with a more insular US under the Trump presidency, points to an even greater need for Australia to consolidate its future in its own region of the Asia Pacific – and, indeed, in the wider arena of Asia.

In 2017, the shares of world gross domestic product (GDP) are forecast to be: Asia Pacific (33%); the Indian subcontinent (9%); North America (19%); Central and South America (6%); Western and Central Europe, mainly the EU (17%); Eastern Europe (4%); the Middle East (7%); and Africa (5%). These are higher shares than thought for the two Asian regions just 18 months ago.

2016 was a landmark year in that it was the first time the East passed the GDP of the West – at least in purchasing power parity (PPP) terms, which is the most important measure of economic size. This year, Asia will top 42% of the world's GDP, passing Europe and North America combined.

Asia's economic composition in 2017 and its growth prospects are shown in the two charts on the next page; the giants being China and India.

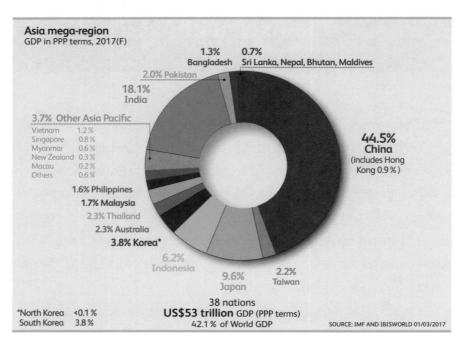

## Asia mega-region
GDP in PPP terms, 2017(F)

- 1.3% Bangladesh
- 0.7% Sri Lanka, Nepal, Bhutan, Maldives
- 2.0% Pakistan
- 18.1% India
- 3.7% Other Asia Pacific
  - Vietnam 1.2%
  - Singapore 0.8%
  - Myanmar 0.6%
  - New Zealand 0.3%
  - Macau 0.2%
  - Others 0.6%
- 1.6% Philippines
- 1.7% Malaysia
- 2.3% Thailand
- 2.3% Australia
- 3.8% Korea*
- 6.2% Indonesia
- 9.6% Japan
- 2.2% Taiwan
- 44.5% China (includes Hong Kong 0.9%)

*North Korea <0.1%
South Korea 3.8%

38 nations
**US$53 trillion** GDP (PPP terms)
42.1% of World GDP

SOURCE: IMF AND IBISWORLD 01/03/2017

## Asia growth 2017 (F)
Major Asia Pacific and Indian subcontinent nations (PPP ranking)

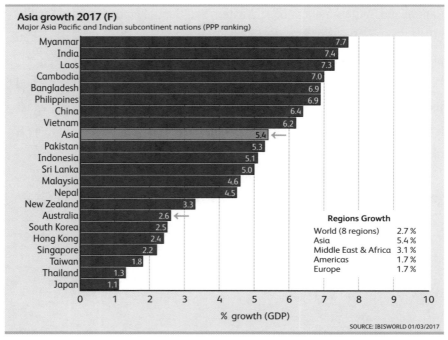

| Nation | % growth (GDP) |
|---|---|
| Myanmar | 7.7 |
| India | 7.4 |
| Laos | 7.3 |
| Cambodia | 7.0 |
| Bangladesh | 6.9 |
| Philippines | 6.9 |
| China | 6.4 |
| Vietnam | 6.2 |
| Asia | 5.4 |
| Pakistan | 5.3 |
| Indonesia | 5.1 |
| Sri Lanka | 5.0 |
| Malaysia | 4.6 |
| Nepal | 4.5 |
| New Zealand | 3.3 |
| Australia | 2.6 |
| South Korea | 2.5 |
| Hong Kong | 2.4 |
| Singapore | 2.2 |
| Taiwan | 1.8 |
| Thailand | 1.3 |
| Japan | 1.1 |

**Regions Growth**

| Region | Growth |
|---|---|
| World (8 regions) | 2.7% |
| Asia | 5.4% |
| Middle East & Africa | 3.1% |
| Americas | 1.7% |
| Europe | 1.7% |

SOURCE: IBISWORLD 01/03/2017

Australia is tiny, at 2.3% of the region's GDP; yet that still places us as the 19th largest economy in the world of 230 nations and protectorates, with 1% of world GDP (PPP terms). Tinier still is our population of 24.5 million, which makes up just 0.3% of the world population of 7.4 billion.

The next table further reminds us of our smallness among Asia's economic and populated giants in everything except land mass.

### Australia's major Asian neighbours
2017

| Nation | Land Mass (million km²) | Population (million) | Density (persons/km²) | GDP ($US billion, PPP) |
|--------|--------|--------|--------|--------|
| Australia | 7.7 | 24 | 3 | 1.3 |
| Indonesia | 1.9 | 258 | 137 | 3.3 |
| Philippines | 0.3 | 103 | 337 | 0.9 |
| Vietnam | 0.3 | 95 | 95 | 0.7 |
| Thailand | 0.5 | 68 | 68 | 1.2 |
| China | 9.6 | 1373 | 143 | 23.1 |
| South Korea | 0.1 | 51 | 507 | 2.0 |
| Japan | 0.4 | 127 | 870 | 5.1 |
| India | 3.3 | 1267 | 399 | 9.6 |

SOURCE: IBISWORLD 01/03/2017

And the exhibit below shows the degree of our scarcity of population.

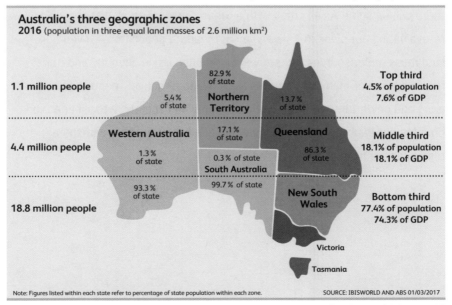

### Australia's three geographic zones
2016 (population in three equal land masses of 2.6 million km²)

1.1 million people

82.9% of state — Northern Territory
5.4% of state
13.7% of state

**Top third**
4.5% of population
7.6% of GDP

4.4 million people

Western Australia
17.1% of state
1.3% of state
Queensland
0.3% of state — South Australia
86.3% of state

**Middle third**
18.1% of population
18.1% of GDP

18.8 million people

93.3% of state
99.7% of state
New South Wales

**Bottom third**
77.4% of population
74.3% of GDP

Victoria

Tasmania

Note: Figures listed within each state refer to percentage of state population within each zone.

SOURCE: IBISWORLD AND ABS 01/03/2017

Our top third, with a land mass of 2.6 million square kilometres, has a population of just over a million people. Our nearest neighbour, Indonesia, with less than three-quarters of that land mass, has a population nearly 250 times greater!

In case we think of the top third of our continent as dry and largely uninhabitable, that part of our land mass holds 60% of our annual water supply.

There are now seven Asian cities that are of a similar or greater population size than our entire nation, with its extraordinary land mass. They include: Tokyo (38 million); Shanghai (34 million); Chongqing (less than 32 million); Jakarta (31 million); Karachi (25 million); Delhi (25 million); and Beijing (25 million). More will follow.

None of these facts should ever lead to xenophobia of the sort Australians have exhibited at various times in our history. We are already on our way to a Eurasian society by the end of this century, having been European in the 20th century and British in the 18th century; and we will be on our way to an Asian society in the 22nd century, albeit a rich and westernised Asian society.

Although we are expected to have a population of 70 million by 2100, there will be some Asian cities with a greater population at that time. So, re-evaluating our place in Asia and an appropriate population – given our land mass and resources – there will be an ongoing neighbourly and moral responsibility for many generations to come. To effectively contribute to such a big and powerful part of the world economy and society, we will need to broaden our thinking to consider how we can better utilise – and share – the resources we have available in Australia.

The year 2017 is likely to be the most turbulent since 2009, when the GFC was in full swing; except this time it includes political, racial, religious and terrorist issues more than finance and economic ones. Not that the latter issues have gone away either; just sublimated by the other issues for the time being.

But financial and economic issues are fellow travellers with socio-political issues. Economic and financial hegemony from the Western world certainly played a part in the religious, terrorist and political upheavals of the late 20th and early 21st centuries. Greed and corruption in corporations and governments has become rampant since the turn of this new century, in both developed and emerging countries.

Religion – especially Islam – began to be used as a weapon in Middle Eastern, Central Asian and North African countries against Western nations, and sometimes on an internecine basis within Islamic cultures. Visionless, gormless and often timorous governments added to the cocktail, exacerbating the growing crises. So, it is worthwhile looking at the issues that are part of current dysfunctionality: globalisation and regionalisation, changing economic power structures, religious terrorism, the USA's dilemma and changing political ideologies.

## Globalisation and regionalisation

The world has been regionalising more than globalising in the new age since 1965; with the world's 230 nations and protectorates gradually forming eight trading if not sovereign regions.

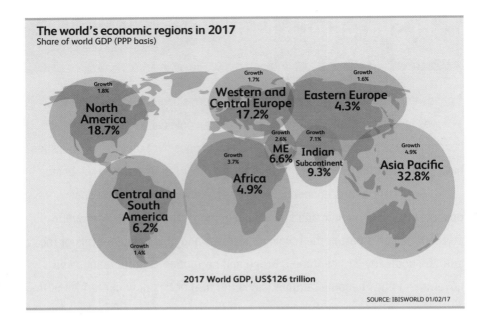

**The world's economic regions in 2017**
Share of world GDP (PPP basis)

Growth
1.8%
North
America
18.7%

Growth
1.7%
Western and
Central Europe
17.2%

Growth
1.6%
Eastern Europe
4.3%

Growth
2.6%
ME
6.6%

Growth
7.1%
Indian
Subcontinent
9.3%

Growth
4.9%
Asia Pacific
32.8%

Growth
3.7%
Africa
4.9%

Central and
South
America
6.2%

Growth
1.4%

2017 World GDP, US$126 trillion

SOURCE: IBISWORLD 01/02/17

This is more pronounced than globalisation in economic significance, although capital flows have certainly assumed a free-wheeling global pattern. Multinational corporations have also been significant and are often seen as colonising cultures across the globe. But full political and economic globalisation awaits the tail end of this 21$^{st}$ century. These forces have alarmed societies with their speed as well as their penetration.

## Changing economic power

In the chart above, the dominance of Asia — being a combination of the Asia Pacific and the Indian subcontinent — is obvious with 42% of world gross domestic product (GDP). It already exceeds the size of Western and Central Europe and North America combined (36%). Indeed, in 2016, the East overtook the West in GDP terms for the first time, so the new world order is being changed early in this 21$^{st}$ century.

The chart on the next page reinforces this power shift. China's GDP is now over a third larger than that of the United States and India is now almost double the size of Japan, and more than double the size of Germany. Brazil and Indonesia have well and truly overtaken the United Kingdom, which is nowadays only just over double the GDP of Australia.

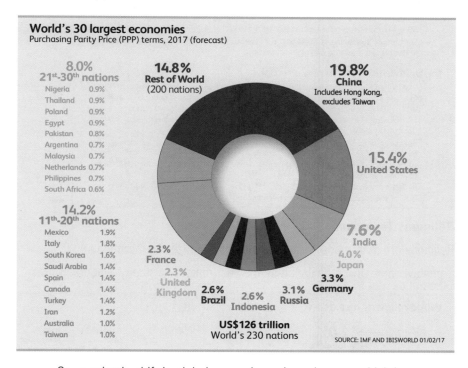

**World's 30 largest economies**
Purchasing Parity Price (PPP) terms, 2017 (forecast)

| 8.0% 21st-30th nations | |
|---|---|
| Nigeria | 0.9% |
| Thailand | 0.9% |
| Poland | 0.9% |
| Egypt | 0.9% |
| Pakistan | 0.8% |
| Argentina | 0.7% |
| Malaysia | 0.7% |
| Netherlands | 0.7% |
| Philippines | 0.7% |
| South Africa | 0.6% |

| 14.2% 11th-20th nations | |
|---|---|
| Mexico | 1.9% |
| Italy | 1.8% |
| South Korea | 1.6% |
| Saudi Arabia | 1.4% |
| Spain | 1.4% |
| Canada | 1.4% |
| Turkey | 1.4% |
| Iran | 1.2% |
| Australia | 1.0% |
| Taiwan | 1.0% |

**14.8%** Rest of World (200 nations)

**19.8%** China Includes Hong Kong, excludes Taiwan

**15.4%** United States

**7.6%** India

**4.0%** Japan

**3.3%** Germany

**3.1%** Russia

**2.6%** Indonesia

**2.6%** Brazil

**2.3%** France

**2.3%** United Kingdom

**US$126 trillion** World's 230 nations

SOURCE: IMF AND IBISWORLD 01/02/17

So, a seismic shift in global power is again underway, which is unsettling to those who had the power – and prestige – and do not want to relinquish it. Those who now hold the power are not yet experienced in using it; and the peoples of all nations are unsettled in the process.

## Our two historical allies are losing power

Australia, not quite 230 years old as a modern and now developed economy, has depended heavily on the United States and the United States: the United States for some 140 years of that time, and the United States for the rest.

But both are now under pressure from outside and inside their own nations, as suggested in the following summary.

## A tale of two long-standing allies

### The **United Kingdom** and **Brexit**

- In the post-Industrial Age (our Infotronics Age, since 1965), nations have been coalescing into trading or sovereign regions for peace, economies-of-scale and trading benefits. For the United Kingdom to go it alone with just 2.25% of world GDP is an emotional (read: irrational) decision. For the decision to be based on getting just over 50% in a non-compulsory voting regime is crazy.
- You cannot fly solo in the world of the 21st century; strategic alliances are survival kits in this big regionalising and globalising century.

### The **United States** and its **new direction**

- The United States is in serious long-term trouble. It has run a positive Budget for just four years over the past 40 or more years. It has had the biggest debt build-up since WWII. Despite leading the world in post-Industrial industries (health, pharmaceutical, IT, material sciences etc.), there are regressive forces trying to keep old industries past their use-by date.
- But greed, polarisation of wealth, unpunished financial criminality and undemocratic election systems (electoral college) — where a candidate with almost 2.9 million more votes loses to the opponent who becomes a legal but illegitimate President — all point to serious problems.
- In 2016, the GDP of the East (dominated by China and a rising India) overtook the GDP of the West. The Rubicon has been crossed.

SOURCE: IBISWORLD 01/02/17

# Religious Terrorism

Religions are man-made of course, albeit with altruistic intentions and, arguably, some divine guidance by the vast majority of their founders. But as

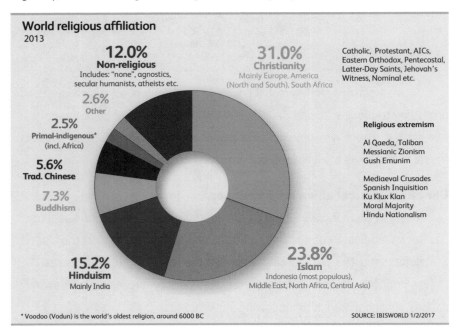

**World religious affiliation**
2013

**12.0%**
**Non-religious**
Includes: "none", agnostics, secular humanists, atheists etc.

**31.0%**
**Christianity**
Mainly Europe, America
(North and South), South Africa

Catholic, Protestant, AICs, Eastern Orthodox, Pentecostal, Latter-Day Saints, Jehovah's Witness, Nominal etc.

**2.6%**
Other

**2.5%**
Primal-indigenous*
(incl. Africa)

**5.6%**
**Trad. Chinese**

**7.3%**
Buddhism

**Religious extremism**

Al Qaeda, Taliban
Messianic Zionism
Gush Emunim

Mediaeval Crusades
Spanish Inquisition
Ku Klux Klan
Moral Majority
Hindu Nationalism

**15.2%**
**Hinduism**
Mainly India

**23.8%**
**Islam**
Indonesia (most populous),
Middle East, North Africa, Central Asia)

* Voodoo (Vodun) is the world's oldest religion, around 6000 BC

SOURCE: IBISWORLD 1/2/2017

the famed author Karen Armstrong has posed in her landmark book, *The Battle for God*, which one is the true God? Clearly this question has been the stuff of feuds, fights, terrible wars and terrorism. All of these are also man-made and are an abomination of the original founders' teachings.

It just happens to be the fringe dwellers of Islam's turn to do terrible things – another frightening element of the second decade we are in, and a major reason for the tizz we are in.

## The USA and the post-GFC

The most unsettling element in the developed world, and the West in particular, is undoubtedly the USA situation as 2017 unfolds. The chart below shows the history of the US GDP growth over the past nine decades.

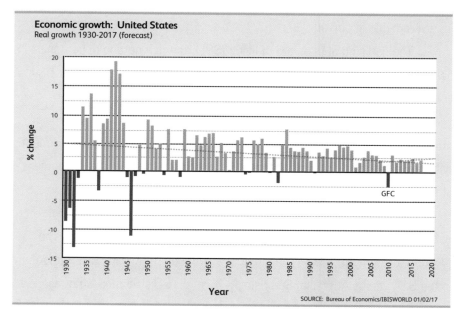

**Economic growth: United States**
Real growth 1930-2017 (forecast)

SOURCE: Bureau of Economics/IBISWORLD 01/02/17

When the GFC struck, the US government, led by President Obama and other heads of state around the world, faced two choices. The first was to have a classical depression for 3-4 years with massive unemployment (15%+), a purging of the financial criminals, a wake-up call to society at large, then a return to normal growth. The second option was to fill the potential hole in with unprecedented pump-priming ('quantitative easing') and spread the pain out over ten years or more with half the normal 3.5% p.a. GDP growth during that 'recovery ward' period.

But halving the GDP growth in the United States and Europe would mean no increase in standard of living for a decade, the trade-off for a depression and its massive unemployment.

World leaders chose the latter: less pain, but with no criminals charged or convicted in the USA, and no wake-up call to society (especially the greedy rich). Governments didn't explain this choice to the electorate, and they let greed and polarisation of incomes continue, all of which lead to a loss of faith in governments in power.

The flatlining of standard of living (SOL), the rich getting richer (chart below) and no GFC criminals brought to justice were the last straws for US voters going to the polls to elect a new president in November 2016.

To a greater or lesser extent, the GFC and other economic and social problems have been problematic around the globe, leading to disenchantment with governments of the day. Voters have responded to strongmen regardless of their qualifications, rationality or truthfulness.

As mentioned earlier, the greed of the entrenched rich has been particularly galling, more so with flatlined incomes among the masses. The next chart (top right) shows the difference between the wealth distribution in the USA versus Australia. Surprisingly, Australia's distribution is not as polarised as most developed economies; but the USA situation has been labelled immoral by most observers.

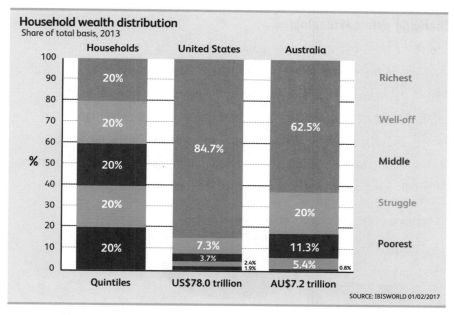

**Household wealth distribution**
Share of total basis, 2013

SOURCE: IBISWORLD 01/02/2017

Of some comfort is the distribution of incomes, as distinct from wealth, as seen below. The closeness of the two countries will surprise most readers; it did this author too.

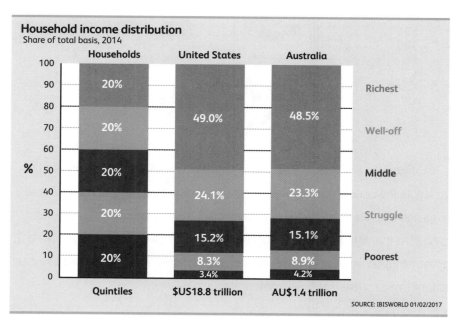

**Household income distribution**
Share of total basis, 2014

SOURCE: IBISWORLD 01/02/2017

## Changing political ideologies

One of the least known developments in politics in the new age, now over 50 years old, is the demise of the old left-right, socialism-capitalism ideological fight of the Industrial age that finished in the developed world in the mid-1960s. The chart below shows two paradigms as they apply to the United States, and a later one shows the Australian situation. Clearly the United States never created a socialist party as such that rose to power, although the term 'left' has been sometimes applied to the Democrats.

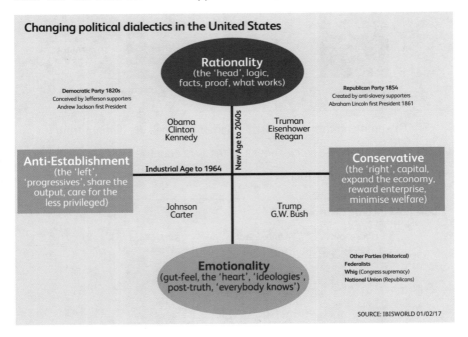

The fight between socialism and capitalism in the Western world virtually ended as the new Infotronics Age of emerging service industry domination and IT gained traction in the mid-1960s. Capitalism had won the fight; and socialists conceded that the means of production would not be owned by the people via government business enterprises (GBEs) and general government, but by private enterprise, because it achieved better outcomes.

However, the business world conceded that higher business taxes would be paid to help the under-privileged, and workers had to be given safer working conditions, greater care and respect. It is ironic that the 'people' are increasingly owning the means of production anyway, via the growing superannuation pools in many developed economies – especially in Australia.

Politics today is driven by either rational (fact-based) or irrational (emotion-based) thinking. Rationality will win in this new age, as did capitalism in the previous Industrial Age, otherwise all the tertiary education, the information explosion and AI software will all have failed; and it won't. But not yet, and not for some years to come.

The Australian situation is depicted in the following exhibit:

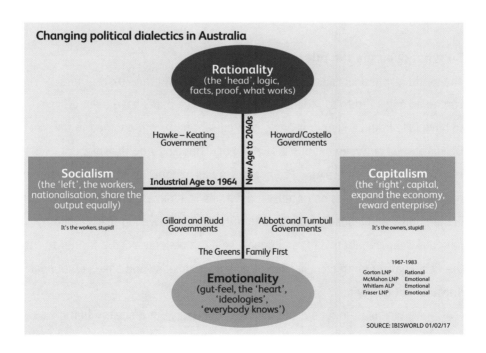

The irrational strongmen are currently in charge across many nations; by default, as already suggested. Weak and irrational previous heads of state, are being swept aside.

In the case of the United States, the circumstances are somewhat different. Hillary Clinton outvoted Donald Trump by 2.9 million votes in the November 2016 Election, and so clearly is the legitimate President. But presidents in the US are not elected by the people, but by the Electoral College; so Donald Trump is the legal; if illegitimate, President. And Obama as the previous President is already being assessed by many analysts as one of the 10 best Presidents of the 44 so far until Donald Trump – but not without some criticisms, albeit mitigated by a hostile Congress during his period in office.

## So what does the the future hold?

The world is into uncharted waters as we progress into the 2020s. There can be no quick return to rationality until alternative paths have been proven to have failed; and if history is any guide, current paths *are* doomed to fail. Building walls between nations is Hunting and Trapping Age thinking; not sensible in our Infotronic Age. Protectionism has historically left a bleak trail. Racial discrimination inside or between nations is inhuman, breaches basic human rights and leads to wars and more terrorism. Lowering taxes when a nation is deep in debt is daft; and doubly so if the benefits accrue further to the rich. Leaving strategic alliances to go solo in this day and age is emotional bravado, not bravura.

We will need to repeat the mistakes of history, for a society that hasn't experienced it or read enough about it, before sanity and rationality is restored – which will happen.

In the interim, the following summary takes a stab at the next five years.

---

### The next five years: the search for rationality

- Voters around the world have become fed up with greed, financial criminality (unpunished), corruption (government and corporate), stalled living standard growth since the GFC, polarisation of wealth and visionless, gormless and tremulous governments.

- This has paved the way for the emergence of strongmen and emotionality, rather than leaders and rationality: evident in Russia, the United States, Turkey, the Philippines and China. It has its precedents, the last time being the 1930s with Russia, Germany, Italy and Japan.

- The lessons of history once again are either not known or ignored by voters and the new 'saviours'.

- Fortunately, Australia is more a bystander than a participant in the above dilemma. We have minimal national debt; our income and wealth polarisation has not widened this century; we trade in Asia, not the West; we have negligible racial tensions by developed nation standards; and political irrationality is mainly confined in our undemocratically elected Senate.

- That said, we have not had good government for 10 years, with none in sight.

SOURCE: IBISWORLD 01/02/17

---

In short, we should be thankful we live, invest and work in Australia, despite its faults!

# Australia's Prospects in a Weird World

*Company Director* magazine January 2017

Global discombobulation seems to be the order of the day as we face 2017. Bizarre politics, terrorism, mistruths about free trade and globalisation to scare the nervous, digital disruption changing nearly everything – just as electricity did more than a century earlier – and polarised incomes and wealth are all making a lot of the world's 7.4 billion population fearful. It has been a strange 2016, with no guarantee that 2017 will be any more sane.

As we open a new calendar year, the world economy is slowing a little, to an expected 2.6% growth in gross domestic product (GDP), but not collapsing. It is polarised in terms of growing versus stalled economies, and sharing a widespread shortage of statesmen or stateswomen. Vision, hope, courage and leadership are in short supply. Where it does exist, leaders often face internal criticism, as we see in Germany. Others, like New Zealand and Canada, have bold and popular leaders.

## A world in turmoil

In the US, the choice for president was between the unpalatable and the unacceptable. Non-compulsory voting meant that, of some 250 million eligible voters, less than 60% did vote. Those that did voted for change from the politics of recent times – and for a self-proclaimed demigod in the form of Donald Trump, whose many promises are impossible to implement. The old saying, 'be careful what you wish for', may prove prophetic. The US, if not the world, is entering uncharted waters.

Sabre-rattling – a well-known distraction technique when an economy is not going well – surfaced in North Asia and Eastern Europe in 2016. The UK filed for divorce from the moribund EU federation of Central and Western

European economies, and divorces are usually painful. The Philippines elected as president a strongman with 19th century solutions to crime: in this case, drugs.

Much of South America reflected its traditional heady cocktail of politics, class warfare and volatile economics. Economic collapse in Venezuela, negative growth in Brazil and Argentina's GDP, and slow growth elsewhere meant it was not a happy year for the region.

Africa is a mixed bag, as usual, with honest and competent governments and strong economic growth present in only a minority of its 49 nations.

The Middle East continues to be a regrettable mess of Western interference (well-meant or self-seeking), tribalism, internecine religious hatred, civil war and human tragedy in huge numbers: millions. Low oil prices are exacerbating the situation, meaning nations, including even Saudi Arabia, are unable to balance their budgets.

Our own Asia Pacific region, is the best placed of the world's eight geographic regions; more so if we include the Indian subcontinent nations to make up the bigger Asian megaregion which is growing at more than double the world's growth of around 2.7%. Three quarters of our trade, immigration and tourism takes place in this megaregion, so we are well integrated. It is the world's largest economic region at 42% of world GDP, and is the fastest growing at almost 6% in GDP in 2016 and continuing into 2017 at over 5.5%. It is also the most populous region, accounting for 57% of the world's population.

Yes, prices of Australian minerals — going mostly to Asia — have taken a steep dive in recent years, and are now recovering a little; but volumes have continued to grow, and are likely to do so into the late 2020s. If we could only get our act together and attract more than the tiny 1% of Chinese tourists travelling overseas that we do now, our tourism receipts could challenge our total mineral earnings within a decade or so. After all, services are the world's fastest growing traded products. All of which leads to Australia's prospects in 2017.

## What about Australia?

Given that we are in a market-led economy in the post-industrial age of the past half century, rather than the preceding period of supplier-hegemony, it is important to start with the marketplace. The main aggregates are shown in the below chart.

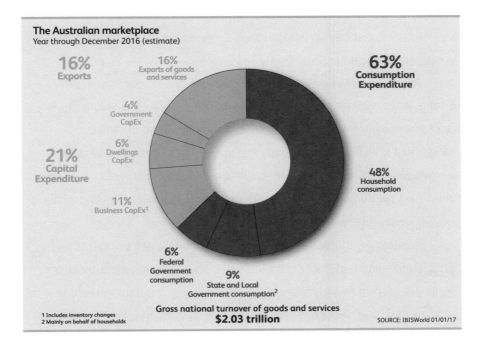

**The Australian marketplace**
Year through December 2016 (estimate)

16% Exports

16% Exports of goods and services

63% Consumption Expenditure

4% Government CapEx

6% Dwellings CapEx

21% Capital Expenditure

48% Household consumption

11% Business CapEx[1]

6% Federal Government consumption

9% State and Local Government consumption[2]

1 Includes inventory changes
2 Mainly on behalf of households

**Gross national turnover of goods and services**
**$2.03 trillion**

SOURCE: IBISWorld 01/01/17

Consumption expenditure dominates, accounting for more than 60% of the total market. Consumption expenditure has not declined in any year during the past six decades and, therefore, has never caused a recession. It won't decline in 2017 either, with expected growth of just under 3%. Exports, accounting for a sixth of the market, very rarely turn negative. These have been growing at more than 6% per year for several years, have never caused a recession in living memory, and should stay at over 4% in 2017.

This leaves capital expenditure – easily the most volatile segment, and the only one that causes recessions – making up more than a fifth of the market. But to cause a recession, total capital expenditure (capex) has to fall more than 8% in a single year. It was down around 4.5% in 2016, and is unlikely to sink to minus 8% in the 2017 financial year, but could do so in either the 2017 calendar year or the 2018 financial year. However, it doesn't have to if the fall in mining capex and probable easing of housing capex (during 2017) are offset by investment in infrastructure by governments and a lift in private investment in equipment and IP.

Any recession is more likely in the 2018 financial year than in 2017. In some ways, we need a recession as a wake-up call for the failure of successive governments to address much-needed reform of the labour market, fast broadband connectivity and speed, fiscal and taxation policy, energy policy, and parliament. The country needs pragmatic vision and goals, rather than platitudes and rhetoric. We haven't had such a wake-up call since 1982–83 and 1992, well over a generation ago.

Fortunately, the nation has a war-chest of past achievements and continuing luck to underpin such temporal disruption and pain if these issues are tackled. It includes our standard of living, our most-liveable cities, consumer and business confidence, relatively tension-free and harmonious society, low national debt, near-full employment and the fact that we are creating well over six times more new jobs than we are losing every five years. We just need visionary, pragmatic and courageous leadership at federal and state levels. We have some shortfalls, as do a lot of countries in this weird world of ours; but hopefully we will get there – without the need for a recession.

# The 2016 US Election in Perspective

*IBISWorld Newsletter* December 2016

The 8 November Election for the US Congress and President came at an interesting point in history. The economy of Western countries, led by the US in the 20th century, was overtaken by that of Eastern countries in early 2016. The US is in no hurry to hand over the leader's baton of the West to China as leader of the East, and indeed is reluctant to ever hand it over. England didn't want to a century ago either, or Rome over a millennium and a half before that.

But China is now the world's biggest economy and the most populous nation, by the proverbial country mile. The pecking order of the G10 and other nations is shown below.

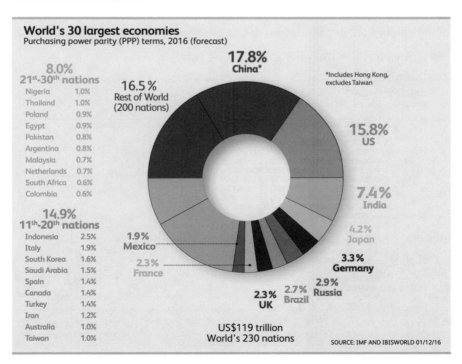

**World's 30 largest economies**
Purchasing power parity (PPP) terms, 2016 (forecast)

**17.8%** China*

*Includes Hong Kong, excludes Taiwan

**16.5 %** Rest of World (200 nations)

**15.8%** US

**7.4%** India

**8.0%** 21st-30th nations

| | |
|---|---|
| Nigeria | 1.0% |
| Thailand | 1.0% |
| Poland | 0.9% |
| Egypt | 0.9% |
| Pakistan | 0.8% |
| Argentina | 0.8% |
| Malaysia | 0.7% |
| Netherlands | 0.7% |
| South Africa | 0.6% |
| Colombia | 0.6% |

**14.9%** 11th-20th nations

| | |
|---|---|
| Indonesia | 2.5% |
| Italy | 1.9% |
| South Korea | 1.6% |
| Saudi Arabia | 1.5% |
| Spain | 1.4% |
| Canada | 1.4% |
| Turkey | 1.4% |
| Iran | 1.2% |
| Australia | 1.0% |
| Taiwan | 1.0% |

**1.9%** Mexico

**2.3%** France

**4.2%** Japan

**3.3%** Germany

**2.9%** Russia

**2.7%** Brazil

**2.3%** UK

US$119 trillion
World's 230 nations

SOURCE: IMF AND IBISWORLD 01/12/16

In 2016, the US's gross domestic product (GDP) is expected to be around US$18.9 trillion, and its net worth around $132.0 trillion. China's GDP is expected to be around US$21.0 trillion in PPP terms, and its net worth around $150.0 trillion, again in PPP terms. That said, China's population of 1.36 billion is more than four times larger than the US's population of 325.1 million, so the per capita situation is poles apart.

By the end of 2016, the US standard of living is expected to be US$58,000 per capita, versus China's US$15,300 per capita. Wealth per capita in the US is likely to be US$406,000 versus US$107,000 for China.

China's infrastructure is newer of course, and better in most cases; although the military might of the US is enormous and dwarfs China's. But not forever.

Both nations have been living beyond their means of late and building up debt: corporate debt in the case of China, and national debt in the case of the US. That said, the government of China is almost bound to stand behind much of the corporate debt. The following charts show comparative debt and budget deficit levels, respectively.

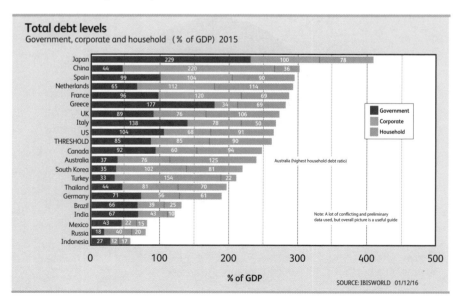

**Total debt levels**
Government, corporate and household (% of GDP) 2015

SOURCE: IBISWORLD 01/12/16

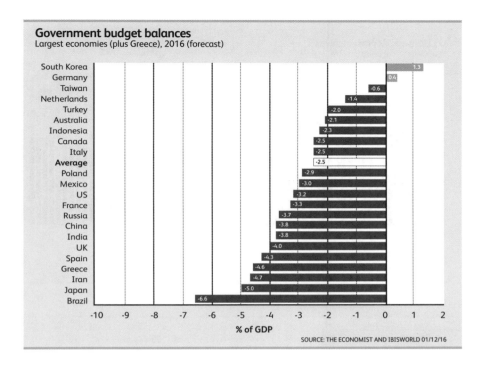

**Government budget balances**
Largest economies (plus Greece), 2016 (forecast)

| Country | % of GDP |
|---|---|
| South Korea | 1.3 |
| Germany | 0.4 |
| Taiwan | -0.6 |
| Netherlands | -1.4 |
| Turkey | -2.0 |
| Australia | -2.1 |
| Indonesia | -2.3 |
| Canada | -2.5 |
| Italy | -2.5 |
| Average | -2.5 |
| Poland | -2.9 |
| Mexico | -3.0 |
| US | -3.2 |
| France | -3.3 |
| Russia | -3.7 |
| China | -3.8 |
| India | -3.8 |
| UK | -4.0 |
| Spain | -4.3 |
| Greece | -4.6 |
| Iran | -4.7 |
| Japan | -5.0 |
| Brazil | -6.6 |

**% of GDP**

SOURCE: THE ECONOMIST AND IBISWORLD 01/12/16

However, the US has been living way beyond its means for a very long time, and spending a very low percentage of its Gross National Expenditure on investment. This has resulted in tired infrastructure. Their world-leading ICT sector isn't enough in this regard.

So, a new Republican President has been elected to take charge in January 2017 with a mostly supportive Congress, which is dominated by Republicans in both houses.

The following three charts trace the election history of the Congress and presidency since the beginning of the 20th century up to the most recent election. These charts reveal that the Democrats have dominated the houses of Congress (> 55% of the time), while the Republicans have won the presidency more often (60% of the time).

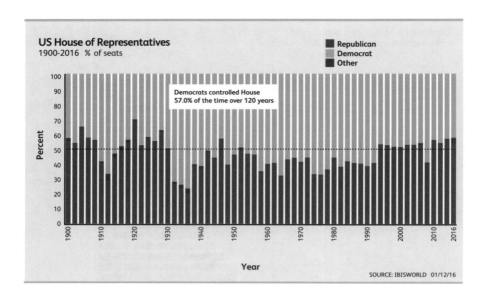

**US House of Representatives**
1900-2016  % of seats

Legend: Republican, Democrat, Other

Democrats controlled House
57.0% of the time over 120 years

Year

SOURCE: IBISWORLD  01/12/16

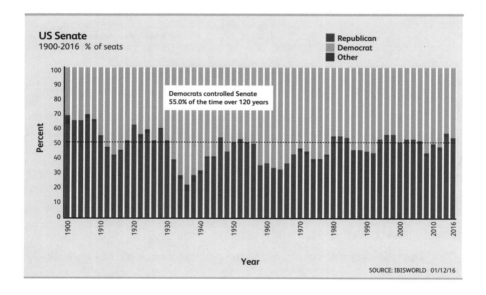

**US Senate**
1900-2016  % of seats

Legend: Republican, Democrat, Other

Democrats controlled Senate
55.0% of the time over 120 years

Year

SOURCE: IBISWORLD  01/12/16

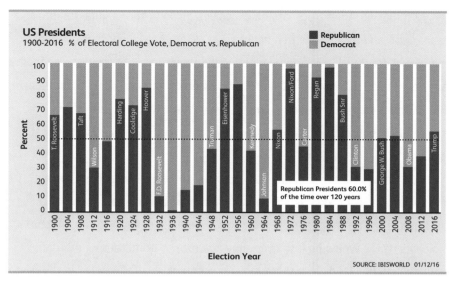

**US Presidents**
1900-2016 % of Electoral College Vote, Democrat vs. Republican

■ Republican
■ Democrat

Republican Presidents 60.0% of the time over 120 years

**Election Year**

SOURCE: IBISWORLD 01/12/16

The incoming President, Donald Trump, will be able to look back on almost half a century to see the nation has balanced its books for only four years (under Clinton's second term), as seen below. Just one-eighth of the past 50 years has balanced or been in surplus. This is serious.

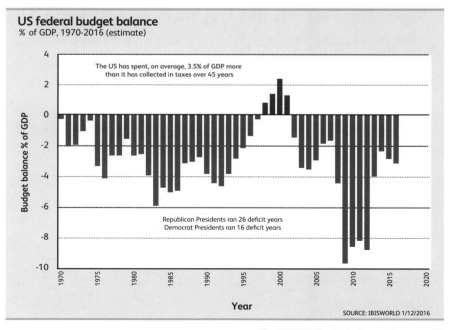

**US federal budget balance**
% of GDP, 1970-2016 (estimate)

The US has spent, on average, 3.5% of GDP more than it has collected in taxes over 45 years

Republican Presidents ran 26 deficit years
Democrat Presidents ran 16 deficit years

**Year**

SOURCE: IBISWORLD 1/12/2016

If making America great again involves going further and faster into more debt, and making the rich richer via tax cuts that favour them, it doesn't augur well for the US. The rich cannot spend their money to grow the economy anyway – due to the small numbers of households and consumer saturation. But with more discretionary income for the vast middleclass, the US would see the GDP grow faster than the lowly few per cent per annum of the past decade.

A great deal of sympathy can be given to the US for its costly world-policeman role over the past 75 years; and a pull-back in some areas is to be expected, if not a greater contribution to defence costs by other nations. However, there would be less sympathy in a retreat from freer world trade, with such action leading to regrettable consequences to all parties in the past.

The real challenge for the US is to avoid what the EU is going through as a big part of the West: a second decline of the Roman Empire, so to speak. The EU has enormous problems including: a divorce (Brexit); high taxes; excessive and restrictive legislation; less than visionary and competent leadership; ageing populations; competition from emerging economies in the industrial era industries; and the need to understand what the new and so-prospective Infotronics Age is all about, let alone another new age due in just several decades.

A lot of the above applies to the US.

Fortunately for Australia, we are now part of the evolving domination by the East, having enjoyed the last several centuries as part of the West, with over three-quarters of our trade, immigration and tourism now in the Asian mega-region (Asia Pacific and the Indian subcontinent).

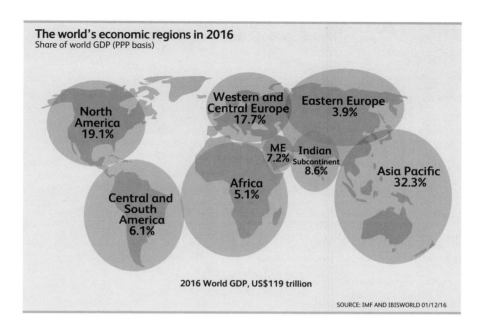

**The world's economic regions in 2016**
Share of world GDP (PPP basis)

North America
19.1%

Western and Central Europe
17.7%

Eastern Europe
3.9%

ME
7.2%

Indian Subcontinent
8.6%

Asia Pacific
32.3%

Africa
5.1%

Central and South America
6.1%

2016 World GDP, US$119 trillion

SOURCE: IMF AND IBISWORLD 01/12/16

A lucky country indeed. But we have reform, vision and leadership issues too. Yes, we have a healthier fiscal base than the US from which to fix these, but we are in a fast growing, competitive and sometimes impatient region. We should be trying harder.

# Urban Myths Versus the Right Information

*IBISWorld Newsletter* November 2016

American corporates on the NYSE have been the world's most profitable, on a weighted-average basis, in the post-Industrial Age over the past half century. The average American company's profitability has been four times the long-term bond rate, which continued through the global financial crisis and beyond. In contrast, Australian companies' average profitability on the ASX has only been twice the 10-year bond rate, apart from during the recent short-lived mining boom.

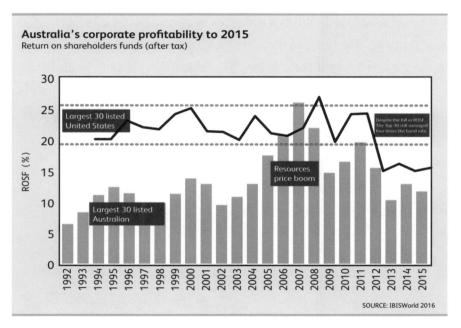

**Australia's corporate profitability to 2015**
Return on shareholders funds (after tax)

SOURCE: IBISWorld 2016

One of the reasons for this discrepancy, perhaps the most important, has been that American corporates spend more on information than any other nation; indeed, twice the gross domestic product (GDP) share of the world's most developed nations. Evidenced-based decisions beat guesswork and gut-feel.

Facts usually ruin good stories, as we know, at work and in our social life. But rumours, scuttlebutt, scandals and old wives' tales can be very believable, and we tend to believe a lot of them until they are debunked. After all, they are interesting, entertaining and often comforting.

But when leading a business or governing a nation, it is safer to make evidence-based decisions, which leads to a number of myths that should be given overdue rebuttal. So what are some of these surviving or new myths, beginning with several that are social urban myths rather than business-related fallacies?

## Marriages don't last as long as they used to

Not true, the average length of a marriage has stayed around 20 years for three centuries. The fact that there are more divorces and separations these days is that we live over twice as long as people did in the early 1800s (when the average lifespan was 38 years), and have time for a trade-in, if you have a mind to. In the olden days, you married at 18, lived another 20 years together and then went to God before you were 40, on average. There just wasn't enough time for a divorce.

## Crime is on the rise, especially murders

No it isn't. Not only is the murder rate in Australia one of the world's lowest, at under two per 100,000 each year, but it has fallen to record lows over the past five years.

## Speeding is the number one cause of road-based deaths

No, things like distractions, falling asleep and intoxication are. Speed is usually somewhere in the 2nd to 4th most common cause.

## We need a big population to compete in a globalising world

No, we don't. Some 18 of the world's 20 highest standard of living countries have a population lower than Australia's 24 million, and most are less than a third of our population. Only the US and Germany are more populous countries in the top 20.

## Australia's population is getting to the limit of our carrying capacity

That's good for a laugh right around the world, especially in high-density Asia. Our population is so thin we could only just touch hand to hand around the coastline. Indonesia's population, on a fraction of our land, could do so 11 deep, and China with only a slightly bigger land mass than us could be 52 deep. On our present growth rate, we will have a population of over 40 million in 2050, and over 75 million by 2100, and still have one of the world's lowest population densities.

## Immigrants take our jobs

No they don't. They more often take jobs we don't like. And if a migrant family arrives, they create demand for more jobs than they can fill for at least five years, in terms of the necessary infrastructure and annual consumption expenditure.

## Australia will run out of workers due to ageing

No we won't. Being too young a population, as we were in the 19th century, was a worse problem; and to get enough workers to support the population, we needed children to start work at under 15 years of age, often as young as 11 to 13. As this century unfolds, working beyond 65 and up to 75 or more – often in a part-time or casual basis – is realistic for a workforce that emphasises brains, not brawn. And the only way to wear the brain out is to stop using it.

## There won't be enough jobs due to technology, robots and artificial intelligence

Yes, there will be. We are good at creating jobs. Over the past five years we have created eight times more jobs than we have lost. Yes, eight times! There are millions of jobs in the making to replace those lost through technology and digital disruption, to be added to our current 12 million jobs.

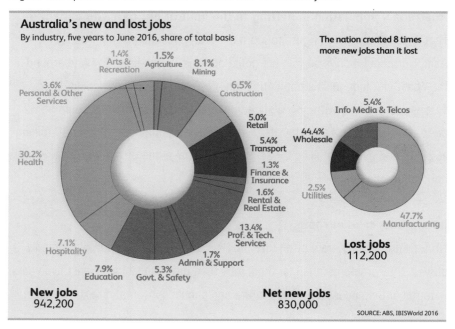

**Australia's new and lost jobs**
By industry, five years to June 2016, share of total basis

The nation created 8 times more new jobs than it lost

- 1.4% Arts & Recreation
- 1.5% Agriculture
- 8.1% Mining
- 3.6% Personal & Other Services
- 6.5% Construction
- 5.0% Retail
- 5.4% Transport
- 30.2% Health
- 44.4% Wholesale
- 1.3% Finance & Insurance
- 1.6% Rental & Real Estate
- 13.4% Prof. & Tech. Services
- 7.1% Hospitality
- 1.7% Admin & Support
- 7.9% Education
- 5.3% Govt. & Safety

**New jobs**
942,200

**Net new jobs**
830,000

- 5.4% Info Media & Telcos
- 2.5% Utilities
- 47.7% Manufacturing

**Lost jobs**
112,200

SOURCE: ABS, IBISWorld 2016

## We are now working harder and with not enough time to scratch ourselves

Not true. For males in the year 1800, it used to be a 65-hour week for 25 years, starting at 13 years of age to complete 80,000 hours of paid work, only to die at an average age of 38. Now it is still 80,000 work hours in a lifetime, but at a pace of less than half those hour per week for longer (more than 50 years); remembering we now have two months off a year through vacations, public holidays and sick leave. We have more discretionary and leisure time than at any time in history.

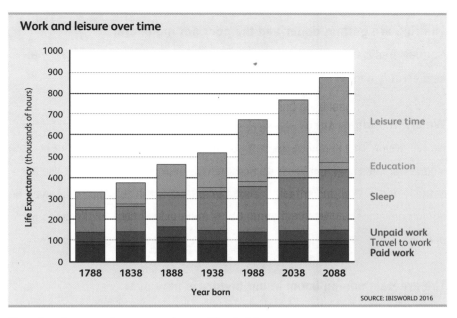

**Work and leisure over time**

Life Expectancy (thousands of hours)

Year born

Leisure time

Education

Sleep

Unpaid work
Travel to work
Paid work

SOURCE: IBISWORLD 2016

## Housing is now dangerously unaffordable

It always was unaffordable for the newlyweds and the poor, so what's new?
Interestingly, the debt servicing ratio (interest payments as a share of disposable income) for mortgage and other debt is currently at the lowest rate in four decades.

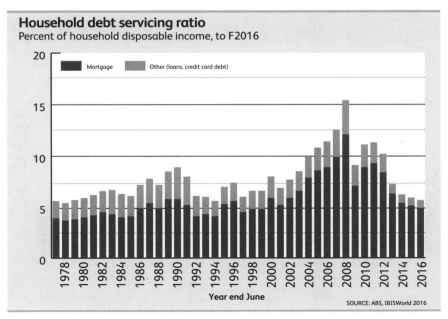

**Household debt servicing ratio**
Percent of household disposable income, to F2016

Mortgage          Other (loans, credit card debt)

Year end June

SOURCE: ABS, IBISWorld 2016

## The rich are getting richer and the poor getting poorer

No they aren't; there has been hardly any change since the beginning of our new century here in Australia.

## We are too-highly taxed

No we aren't. This is one of the most pernicious lies being trundled out by both sides of politics in Australia: blatant scare-mongering and politicking. We are actually one of the lowest taxed developed nations at 28% of GDP. The average among developed countries is around 37% and many nations are nudging 50% of GDP.

## The greatest mining boom in our history is now over

Firstly, it isn't our greatest boom: that was in the 1850s, when the industry reached almost 18% of our GDP – led by gold – versus the current one at just over half that share. And the boom isn't over, production volumes are still growing and may do so well into the 2020s, but boom prices are over.

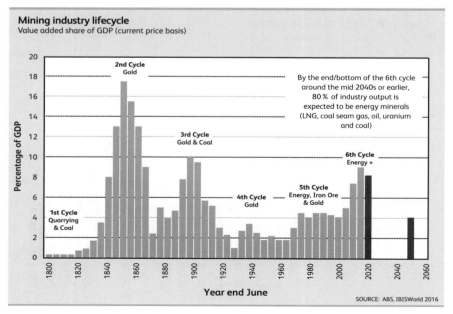

**Mining industry lifecycle**
Value added share of GDP (current price basis)

By the end/bottom of the 6th cycle around the mid 2040s or earlier, 80% of industry output is expected to be energy minerals (LNG, coal seam gas, oil, uranium and coal)

SOURCE: ABS, IBISWorld 2016

## We need to cut costs to balance the budget

Yes, let's regress back to the days when there was no or inadequate support for single mums, the unemployed, the elderly, the disabled or other disadvantaged citizens. Let's not stop till we get back to the 'good old days' when taxes were much lower and may the devil take the hindmost in terms of the people left behind. I don't think so. But, yes, we should get better value for our taxes than we do. One fifth of our GDP is produced by governments, and that sector's productivity has been negative for decades.

## We need to make material things to create basic wealth

No we don't. A wealth creating industry is one that produces products that customers and the market want and are prepared to pay for, regardless of if these products are goods or services. Agriculture, mining, manufacturing and construction are all service industries anyway. Humans didn't create the raw materials on which they are based; God did and they are free. No one has ever been game to take the credit for creating our natural resources, least of all economists and our Bureau of Statistics. The term 'goods industry' is an historical construct to separate tangible from intangible products.

The economy and its wealth is built on value-adding, so wealth creation has only ever been the result of labour, depreciation of capital, indirect taxes and profit going into a product, not the God-given free raw materials.

Agriculture these days creates just 2% of our GDP, and manufacturing less than 6%. In 1960, these two industries were 38%, not 8%! Yet we have a standard of living nearly three times higher than at the end of the Industrial Age in the mid-1960s. If anything, it is our 'service' industries propping up some of the 'goods' industries in this new century.

## Nuclear is the world's most dangerous energy ever used

Wood probably kills more people per kW of energy produced (logging, chopping, asphyxiation, fire). Nuclear energy almost certainly has been the safest energy source on the basis of deaths per kW of energy.

## Australia could become the food bowl of Asia

If only, but we don't have enough water. That said we will probably increase our output fivefold this century as we did in the 20th century, but that will only be enough to feed 5% of Asia's population at the end of the 21st century.

## But despite these myths, are things really getting better?

You bet. Just look at our progress in the chart below.

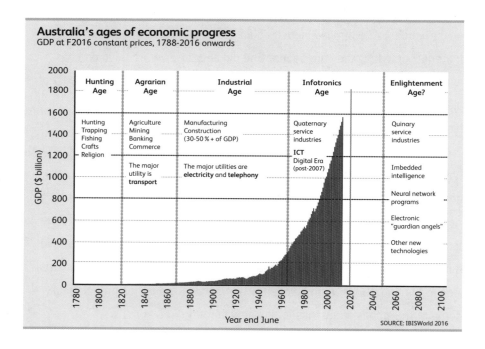

**Australia's ages of economic progress**
GDP at F2016 constant prices, 1788-2016 onwards

And the best is yet to come.

# Our New Federal Government

*IBISWorld Newsletter* September 2016

Running a country these days is not for the faint-hearted. While the problems may vary, the degree of difficulty is high nearly everywhere across the world's 230 nations. If the problem isn't terrorism or racial tensions, it's low economic growth, high debt levels, a high unemployment rate, ecological challenges or the absence of a working majority in government. Sometimes it's all of the above.

Australia elected a new government on 2 July, but we didn't know who was in it – or which party had won – until August. Effectively, the nation has a hung parliament due to the Coalition's slim majority in the House of Representatives, and the minorities-dominated Senate, where no party has control. So, no meaningful reforms will likely be undertaken during the life of this parliament. More's the pity, since we haven't had any reform of significance for a decade. And the clock is ticking on deficits, debt, jobs, productivity, growth, the energy mix, social issues such as same-sex marriage, and more.

The first chart shows the state of the House of Representatives.

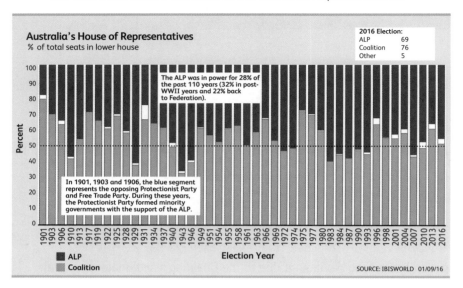

There have only been three other knife-edged parliaments in Australia: in 1940 (United Australian Party), 1961 (Liberal-Country Party) and 2010 (ALP).

Of statistical significance is the fact that the ALP has only governed for around 28% of the time since Federation. This is clearly due to the socialist ideology that underpinned the party, and the ALP only began to revise its platform when capitalism proved to be the better direction by the mid-1960s. The ALP's periods in power have increased to around 45% in the past 50 years. This is due to leadership more than its ideology and union roots, both of which are on an irreversible decline.

The second chart shows the state of the Senate.

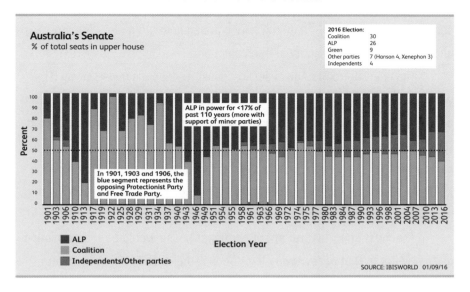

The upper house has been a mess for a very long time. No major party has had a majority since the Fraser Coalition Government in 1977, some 39 years ago. And another majority in the senate is not in sight. Up until 1980, a major party had been in control of the Senate for over 80% of the time. Since then, none of the time.

The Senate does not serve the purpose intended in the 1901 Constitution. It was created as a protector of state rights and powers – given an equal number of seats per state – and a house of review of legislation from the House of Representatives. From inception, the Senate has been an unrepresentative and undemocratic institution, as is the upper house in the British Parliament, the House of Lords. The difference is that the British upper house cannot indefinitely veto legislation from the Commons, only slow it down. Not so with our upper house, once referred to by Paul Keating as 'unrepresentative swill'.

By 1908, the issue of free trade vs. protectionism had been put to bed (in favour of the latter). There were then only two competing ideologies – socialism vs. capitalism – until the new age began in the mid-1960s. So clearly one of the two had a majority at each election.

The new Infotronics Age of service industries (and the underpinning IT), which displaced the Industrial Age, gave rise to a new set of ideologies. We touch on these shortly, but suffice it to say at this point, these new ideologies attracted votes away from the traditional parties, and enabled significant numbers of new senators in the upper house. Indeed, over 26% of all the 72 seats in the recent 2016 election were won by Independents of Other parties. This was aided by the absence of a one-person one-vote democracy for the Senate.

The most important reform of our upper house would be the restriction of its powers to that of reviewing legislation rather than being able to veto bills; although prospects of that change to the Constitution are minimal, as is the creation of representative voting. Again, more's the pity.

This leads us to the new ideologies of the Infotronics age, which have arisen both here and in other developed countries. The next two exhibits summarise the changes.

## The opposing ideologies

**Industrial Age (1860s–1960s)**
- **Socialism vs. Capitalism** (government owns means of production and distribution of income, as oppose to independent ownership and income earned)
- **Compromise at end of this Age:** independent ownership plus triple-bottom-line stakeholders, being profits, planet and people (in the role of customers, workers and suppliers).

**Infotronics Age (1960s–2040s)**
- **Rationalism vs. Emotionalism** (evidence-based logic and decisions as oppose to heart and gut-feelings)
- **Compromise at the end of this Age:** much more fact-checking and fact-based decisions aided by ubiquitous AI software and the emergence of big-data, plus ongoing tolerance, if not acceptance of non-belligerent cultures.

SOURCE: IBISWORLD 01/09/16

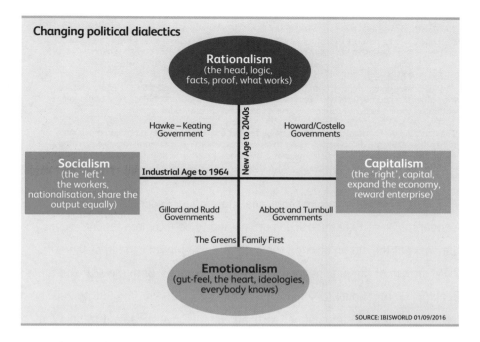

Changing political dialectics

**Rationalism**
(the head, logic, facts, proof, what works)

Hawke – Keating Government

New Age to 2040s

Howard/Costello Governments

**Socialism**
(the 'left', the workers, nationalisation, share the output equally)

Industrial Age to 1964

**Capitalism**
(the 'right', capital, expand the economy, reward enterprise)

Gillard and Rudd Governments

Abbott and Turnbull Governments

The Greens | Family First

**Emotionalism**
(gut-feel, the heart, ideologies, everybody knows)

SOURCE: IBISWORLD 01/09/2016

Australia's dilemma in 2016 is that the governments that have been in power over the past decade have been ensconced in the lower emotional ideological position. And now the ALP and Coalition have the company of The Greens, Family First, the regressive Hansonites and Xenophonites, and a ragtag of independents. All are sitting in the emotional – and often irrational – zone. We can expect no progress of the nation while this situation prevails.

We only need look at two examples of pigheadedness or ideological idiocy to see the blockages to reform and progress as suggested below.

## Roads to nowhere

### Industrial relations
The Work Choices legislation was, in hindsight, the right legislation for the Infotronics Age where worker freedom via contractual relationships without bondage by owners, bosses and unions needed to be progressed. The legislation did need a little more sensitivity, and battled ideological opposition. Sadly, scare-mongering triumphed, despite full employment being restored for the first time in 30 years.

So most are aware of the dismal state of our Federal Government. Neither major party has the vision or courage to do the more rational things that will put the nation back on the path to 3.5% growth instead of the 2.7% growth of the past decade, and full employment. Both the ALP and the Coalition were rational for almost a quarter of a century from 1983 to 2007. Neither are in 2016, and neither party appears to have the talent to take the nation out of the doldrums.

Politicians' spin and spoiling tactics need to be countered by fact-checking, vision and explanations of the benefits of reforms. In the absence of political parties' ability or willingness to do the right thing, businesses and rational social groups need to encourage the media to fulfil this role.

Fortunately, it is businesses that create most of the wealth and jobs each year (around 85%), so the absence of good government is not the end of the world. And our consumer confidence sits around the dividing line of confidence and worry. But it would be nice to have a party in power with rational, visionary and courageous leadership again.

# Australia's Growth Industries

*IBISWorld Newsletter* August 2016

We are told that Australia is the fastest growing economy in the developed world. True, but at 2.7% in the year to March 2016 and the same growth per annum over the past five years, we are not growing as fast as Australia's average over the past 50 years (3.2% per annum) or the 20th century (3.5% per annum). Everyone seems to know the slower growth is due to a lack of reform in our labour market, taxation and parliament, and having the worst broadband speed and capacity in the developed world; a disgrace in an age of digital disruption.

It is small comfort to know that the rest of the developed world is growing slower than we are and has different problems, such as national debt levels, larger government deficits, high taxation, and excessive legislation. And this is less relevant when we realise we are not part of the old rich world of the EU and North America, but are part of Asia. Asia is bigger in gross domestic product (GDP) as well as population than both the EU and North America and is growing three times as fast as they are. And at more than double our speed. Asia is our new economic and demographic arena. That is where we are competing and need to be compared.

But we do have a modern economy in terms of our mix of industries, and we do have growth in enough of them in terms of value added and employment to keep the show on the road.

The first chart on the next page shows the mix of industries as recorded by the ABS in the most recent National Accounts release.

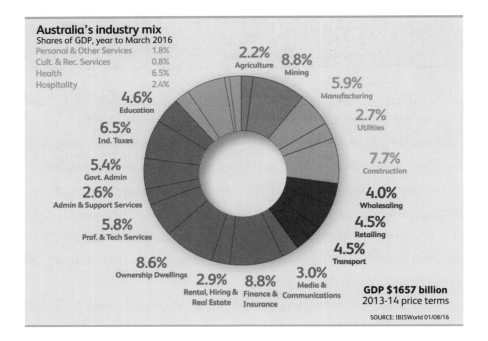

**Australia's industry mix**
Shares of GDP, year to March 2016

| | |
|---|---|
| Personal & Other Services | 1.8% |
| Cult. & Rec. Services | 0.8% |
| Health | 6.5% |
| Hospitality | 2.4% |

4.6% Education

6.5% Ind. Taxes

5.4% Govt. Admin

2.6% Admin & Support Services

5.8% Prof. & Tech Services

8.6% Ownership Dwellings

2.9% Rental, Hiring & Real Estate

8.8% Finance & Insurance

3.0% Media & Communications

2.2% Agriculture

8.8% Mining

5.9% Manufacturing

2.7% Utilities

7.7% Construction

4.0% Wholesaling

4.5% Retailing

4.5% Transport

**GDP $1657 billion**
2013-14 price terms

SOURCE: IBISWorld 01/08/16

It is a mix dominated by service industries, as are all the developed economies of the world. Manufacturing is poised to fall to 5% of our GDP soon, having been almost six times that share at 29% in the early 1960s. However, our standard of living (real GDP/capita) is three times higher than in 1960, so clearly manufacturing has been replaced by more wealth-creating industries.

The two charts on the next page show where the growth has come from over the most recent year and five years, respectively.

It is clear that the only goods-based industries contributing to our growth are mining and, to a lesser extent, construction. Most of our losses are in manufacturing. Mining, of course, has had a horrific fall in prices over the past few years, but volumes (from which real GDP is measured) continue to grow. However, nearly 70% of all growth over the past five years has come from our service industries.

A not-dissimilar picture emerges when we examine the structure and growth of our industries in employment terms.

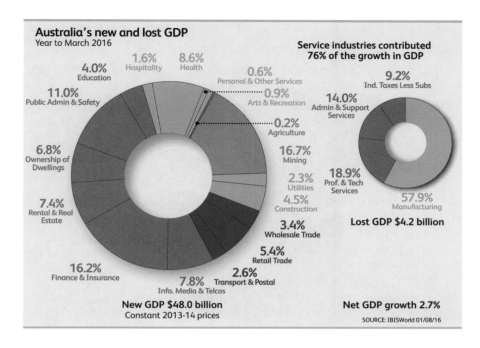

## Australia's new and lost GDP
Year to March 2016

**Service industries contributed 76% of the growth in GDP**

4.0% Education
1.6% Hospitality
8.6% Health
0.6% Personal & Other Services
11.0% Public Admin & Safety
0.9% Arts & Recreation
6.8% Ownership of Dwellings
0.2% Agriculture
7.4% Rental & Real Estate
16.7% Mining
2.3% Utilities
4.5% Construction
16.2% Finance & Insurance
3.4% Wholesale Trade
7.8% Info. Media & Telcos
5.4% Retail Trade
2.6% Transport & Postal

**New GDP $48.0 billion**
Constant 2013-14 prices

9.2% Ind. Taxes Less Subs
14.0% Admin & Support Services
18.9% Prof. & Tech Services
57.9% Manufacturing

**Lost GDP $4.2 billion**

**Net GDP growth 2.7%**

SOURCE: IBISWorld 01/08/16

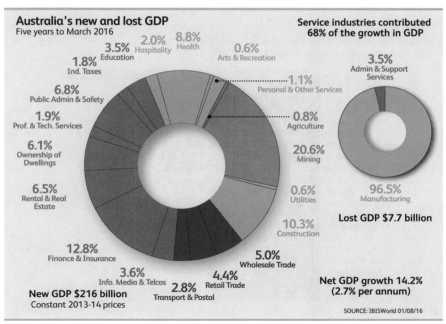

## Australia's new and lost GDP
Five years to March 2016

**Service industries contributed 68% of the growth in GDP**

3.5% Education
2.0% Hospitality
8.8% Health
0.6% Arts & Recreation
1.8% Ind. Taxes
1.1% Personal & Other Services
6.8% Public Admin & Safety
0.8% Agriculture
1.9% Prof. & Tech. Services
20.6% Mining
6.1% Ownership of Dwellings
0.6% Utilities
6.5% Rental & Real Estate
10.3% Construction
12.8% Finance & Insurance
5.0% Wholesale Trade
3.6% Info. Media & Telcos
4.4% Retail Trade
2.8% Transport & Postal

**New GDP $216 billion**
Constant 2013-14 prices

3.5% Admin & Support Services
96.5% Manufacturing

**Lost GDP $7.7 billion**

**Net GDP growth 14.2%**
(2.7% per annum)

SOURCE: IBISWorld 01/08/16

The first chart below shows where our 12 million employees were in March this year, and the second chart reveals what sort of total earnings were being enjoyed in each of the nation's 19 industry divisions as of the 2015 calendar year.

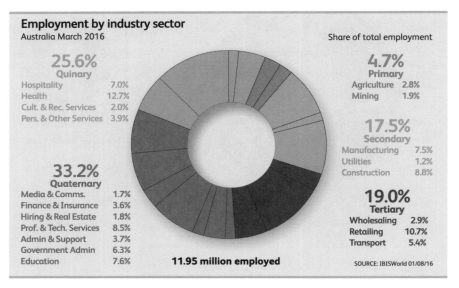

## Employment by industry sector
Australia March 2016

Share of total employment

**25.6%**
Quinary
| | |
|---|---|
| Hospitality | 7.0% |
| Health | 12.7% |
| Cult. & Rec. Services | 2.0% |
| Pers. & Other Services | 3.9% |

**4.7%**
Primary
| | |
|---|---|
| Agriculture | 2.8% |
| Mining | 1.9% |

**17.5%**
Secondary
| | |
|---|---|
| Manufacturing | 7.5% |
| Utilities | 1.2% |
| Construction | 8.8% |

**33.2%**
Quaternary
| | |
|---|---|
| Media & Comms. | 1.7% |
| Finance & Insurance | 3.6% |
| Hiring & Real Estate | 1.8% |
| Prof. & Tech. Services | 8.5% |
| Admin & Support | 3.7% |
| Government Admin | 6.3% |
| Education | 7.6% |

**19.0%**
Tertiary
| | |
|---|---|
| Wholesaling | 2.9% |
| Retailing | 10.7% |
| Transport | 5.4% |

**11.95 million employed**

SOURCE: IBISWorld 01/08/16

## Where the money is by industry
Full-time total adult earnings, December 2015 ($'000)

| Industry | % of workforce | Wages ($'000) |
|---|---|---|
| Mining | 1.9% of workforce | 136.1 |
| Utilities | 1.2% | 96.5 |
| Finance & Insurance | 8.7% | 95.1 |
| Prof. & Tech. Services | 3.3% | 93.0 |
| Info Media & Telcos | 1.9% | 91.7 |
| Construction | 8.8% | 87.4 |
| Transport & Postal | 6.3% | 86.9 |
| Public Admin & Safety | 5.2% | 84.6 |
| Education | 7.8% | 83.2 |
| All industries | | 81.4 |
| Health | 3.4% | 78.0 |
| Wholesale Trade | 12.6% | 76.5 |
| Manufacturing | 7.8% | 76.3 |
| Arts & Recreation | 1.9% | 70.6 |
| Rental & Real Estate Serv. | 3.5% | 70.3 |
| Admin & Support | 1.8% | 67.0 |
| Personal & Other Services | 4.1% | 62.8 |
| Retail Trade | 10.3% | 59.3 |
| Agriculture | 2.5% | 58.0 |
| Hospitality | 7.0% | 54.5 |

Total employed 11.9 million

Wages ($'000)

SOURCE: IBISWorld 01/08/16

Again, it is a nation where service industry jobs dominate the workforce. And contrary to common belief, there are more above-average earnings in the service industries than in the goods-based industries. Manufacturing is well below the national average nowadays; so why do we still have some politicians suggesting we should go back there? Regressive economics.

The good news, which is not publicised enough to a society nervous about jobs for themselves and their children, is that we are creating far more jobs than we are losing. This trend is abundantly clear in the following two charts that cover the year to March 2016 and the five years to the same time.

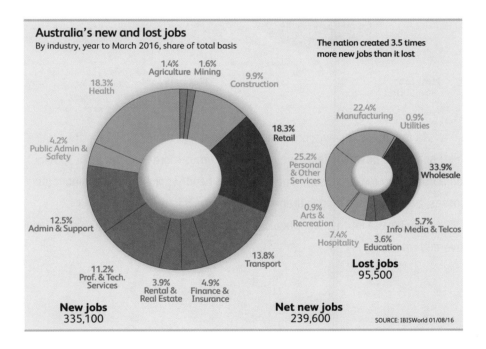

**Australia's new and lost jobs**
By industry, year to March 2016, share of total basis

The nation created 3.5 times more new jobs than it lost

1.4% Agriculture  1.6% Mining
18.3% Health
9.9% Construction
18.3% Retail
4.2% Public Admin & Safety
25.2% Personal & Other Services
12.5% Admin & Support
11.2% Prof. & Tech. Services
3.9% Rental & Real Estate
4.9% Finance & Insurance
13.8% Transport

22.4% Manufacturing  0.9% Utilities
33.9% Wholesale
0.9% Arts & Recreation
5.7% Info Media & Telcos
7.4% Hospitality  3.6% Education

**New jobs** 335,100

**Net new jobs** 239,600

**Lost jobs** 95,500

SOURCE: IBISWorld 01/08/16

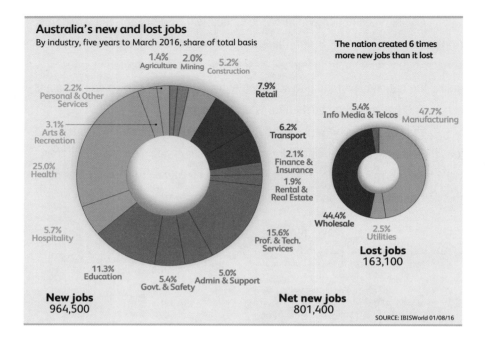

**Australia's new and lost jobs**

By industry, five years to March 2016, share of total basis

The nation created 6 times more new jobs than it lost

1.4% Agriculture
2.0% Mining
5.2% Construction
7.9% Retail
2.2% Personal & Other Services
3.1% Arts & Recreation
25.0% Health
5.7% Hospitality
11.3% Education
5.4% Govt. & Safety
5.0% Admin & Support
15.6% Prof. & Tech. Services
1.9% Rental & Real Estate
2.1% Finance & Insurance
6.2% Transport

**New jobs**
964,500

**Net new jobs**
801,400

5.4% Info Media & Telcos
47.7% Manufacturing
44.4% Wholesale
2.5% Utilities

**Lost jobs**
163,100

SOURCE: IBISWorld 01/08/16

In the latest year, we created three-and-a-half times more jobs than we lost; and in the past five years we created six times more than we lost. So why on earth do we make big song-and-dance and hand-wringing routines about job losses, but practically no celebration about our new jobs?

We have a lot to cheer about, without being complacent about urgent and overdue reforms.

# Australia's 100 Biggest and 100 Best Businesses

*Occasional Paper* May/June 2016

Australia's biggest enterprises are not our best enterprises as we will see shortly, even though there are a dozen world's best practice (WBP) performers among the Biggest 100. In the Best 100, all are at the highest end of WBP. But we begin this analysis with some top-down statistics and trends of all businesses in Australia before focusing on the nation's biggest and best enterprises.

The year 2016 should end with Australia having 2.15 million active trading businesses, generating a gross domestic product (GDP) of almost $1.7 trillion, with revenues of $5 trillion and employing 12.1 million persons.

A guide to the number of businesses in various revenue size categories is shown below. The so-called 'big end of town' is significant. Some 312 enterprises

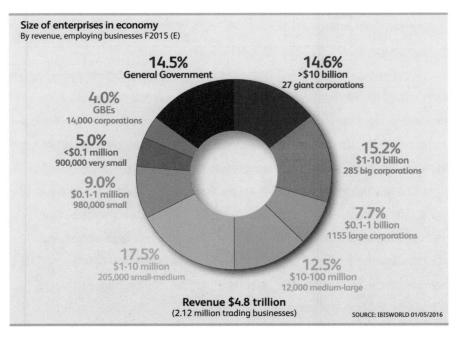

**Size of enterprises in economy**
By revenue, employing businesses F2015 (E)

**14.5%** General Government

**14.6%** >$10 billion — 27 giant corporations

**4.0%** GBEs — 14,000 corporations

**5.0%** <$0.1 million — 900,000 very small

**9.0%** $0.1-1 million — 980,000 small

**15.2%** $1-10 billion — 285 big corporations

**7.7%** $0.1-1 billion — 1155 large corporations

**17.5%** $1-10 million — 205,000 small-medium

**12.5%** $10-100 million — 12,000 medium-large

**Revenue $4.8 trillion**
(2.12 million trading businesses)

SOURCE: IBISWORLD 01/05/2016

with revenues over $1 billion in 2015 accounted for 30% of the nation's $4.8 trillion total revenue. Enterprises with over $10 million in revenue account for just over half all revenue with just 0.6% of the number of businesses, meaning that the Small to Medium Enterprises (SME) sector generates the other half, but with 99.4% of all enterprises.

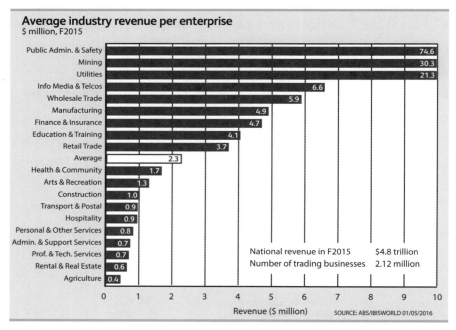

**Average industry revenue per enterprise**
$ million, F2015

| Industry | Revenue ($ million) |
|---|---|
| Public Admin. & Safety | 74.6 |
| Mining | 30.3 |
| Utilities | 21.3 |
| Info Media & Telcos | 6.6 |
| Wholesale Trade | 5.9 |
| Manufacturing | 4.9 |
| Finance & Insurance | 4.7 |
| Education & Training | 4.1 |
| Retail Trade | 3.7 |
| Average | 2.3 |
| Health & Community | 1.7 |
| Arts & Recreation | 1.3 |
| Construction | 1.0 |
| Transport & Postal | 0.9 |
| Hospitality | 0.9 |
| Personal & Other Services | 0.8 |
| Admin. & Support Services | 0.7 |
| Prof. & Tech. Services | 0.7 |
| Rental & Real Estate | 0.6 |
| Agriculture | 0.4 |

National revenue in F2015    $4.8 trillion
Number of trading businesses  2.12 million

Revenue ($ million)          SOURCE: ABS/IBISWORLD 01/05/2016

The SME sector has come a long way since the end of the Industrial Age and the emergence of the new Infotronics Age of service industries and the IT revolution in the mid-1960s. Its share of the nation's revenue 50 years ago was around 30% of the total, but is now almost equal in importance to the big end of town.

Clearly, it has been the SME sector that has pioneered the new service industries via household functions outsourcing, business non-core functions and overseas outsourcing to Australia (tourism, educations business services, etc.). Franchising has been a significant contributor to the faster growth of SMEs not only in new retailing, such as fast food and specialty clothing, but in new household and business services.

The biggest enterprises are mainly clustered into nine of the nation's 19 industry divisions, as can be seen on the chart on the previous page. There are some big corporations in other industries, of course, but such industries are mainly inhabited by SMEs.

## The Biggest 100 Businesses

The nation's Biggest 100 had combined revenues of $1079 billion in 2015, representing a massive 23% of the nation's total revenue that year of $4.8 billion. And they occupied 15 of the nation's 19 industry divisions. Regrettably, their weighted average return on shareholder funds after tax (ROSF) was just 10% over the five-year period to 2015. A lot of commercial property and property trusts – passive investments that they are – did better than this.

Some excuse may lie with the impact of the GFC and lower than average GDP growth, but Australia has had no recession over this period and some serendipity (mining boom and growing inbound tourism) and low interest rates on commercial loans. More telling is that our Best 100, which we explore shortly, had the same economic conditions, were in similar industries and had five-times better average ROSF!

The two following charts are illuminating in this regard. The first shows the profitability ranges of the Biggest 100 over a five-year period to 2015, revealing that there were a large number (18) that ran at a loss over that period, outnumbering those that achieved WBP (12).

The second chart shows the profitability of the 15 industries (of the nation's 19) occupied by the Biggest 100 over the five-year period. Eight of the industries had a lower average ROSF than the already-low average of 10%.

## Profitability of Australia's biggest 100 enterprises

Number, by profitability range. ROSF after tax ( % ), simple averages (five-year average to F2015)

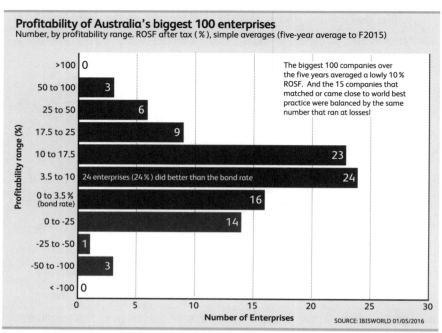

The biggest 100 companies over the five years averaged a lowly 10 % ROSF. And the 15 companies that matched or came close to world best practice were balanced by the same number that ran at losses!

| Profitability range (%) | Number of Enterprises |
|---|---|
| >100 | 0 |
| 50 to 100 | 3 |
| 25 to 50 | 6 |
| 17.5 to 25 | 9 |
| 10 to 17.5 | 23 |
| 3.5 to 10 | 24 enterprises (24 %) did better than the bond rate — 24 |
| 0 to 3.5 % (bond rate) | 16 |
| 0 to -25 | 14 |
| -25 to -50 | 1 |
| -50 to -100 | 3 |
| < -100 | 0 |

SOURCE: IBISWORLD 01/05/2016

## Profitability of Australia's biggest 100 companies[1]

By industry division, return on shareholder funds (after tax), five years to F2015

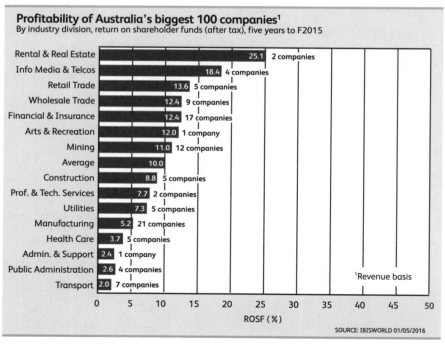

| Industry | ROSF ( % ) | Companies |
|---|---|---|
| Rental & Real Estate | 25.1 | 2 companies |
| Info Media & Telcos | 18.4 | 4 companies |
| Retail Trade | 13.6 | 5 companies |
| Wholesale Trade | 12.4 | 9 companies |
| Financial & Insurance | 12.4 | 17 companies |
| Arts & Recreation | 12.0 | 1 company |
| Mining | 11.0 | 12 companies |
| Average | 10.0 | |
| Construction | 8.8 | 5 companies |
| Prof. & Tech. Services | 7.7 | 2 companies |
| Utilities | 7.3 | 5 companies |
| Manufacturing | 5.2 | 21 companies |
| Health Care | 3.7 | 5 companies |
| Admin. & Support | 2.4 | 1 company |
| Public Administration | 2.6 | 4 companies |
| Transport | 2.0 | 7 companies |

[1]Revenue basis

SOURCE: IBISWORLD 01/05/2016

The next list reveal the Biggest 100 enterprises in Australia in 2015 and their statistics. Those 12 enterprises achieving world best practice (ROSF >20%) are shown in blue, and the 18 loss-makers in red.

## 100 Biggest Australian Enterprises
By ROSF (%), five years to 2015

| Enterprise | ROSF (%) | Revenue ($ billion) | Enterprise | ROSF (%) | Revenue ($ billion) |
|---|---|---|---|---|---|
| 1. TCorp | 67.2 | 4.7 | 54. Mitsubishi Development | 6.4 | 4.7 |
| 2. JB Hi-Fi | 52.2 | 3.7 | 55. Aurizon | 6.2 | 3.8 |
| 3. Apple | 52.0 | 8.0 | 56. ConocoPhillips Australia | 6.0 | 4.1 |
| 4. CSL | 37.2 | 7.3 | 57. Toll Holdings | 5.6 | 8.6 |
| 5. Fortescue Metals Group | 31.2 | 11.3 | 58. AGL | 5.2 | 10.7 |
| 6. Telstra | 28.8 | 26.8 | 59. Suncorp Group | 5.0 | 16.7 |
| 7. Ausgrid | 28.0 | 3.2 | 60. Glencore | 5.0 | 4.4 |
| 8. Brambles | 25.8 | 7.3 | 61. QBE Insurance Group | 4.8 | 23.4 |
| 9. Scentre Group | 25.0 | 2.9 | 62. Rio Tinto | 4.4 | 49.8 |
| 10. Japan Australia | 24.8 | 2.8 | 63. Brookfield Multiplex | 4.0 | 3.9 |
| 11. Woolworths | 23.0 | 61.1 | 64. Seven Group | 4.0 | 3.0 |
| 12. Bidvest | 22.2 | 3.1 | 65. IBM A/NZ Holdings | 3.5 | 3.9 |
| 13. Amcor | 21.0 | 9.8 | 66. EnergyAustralia | 3.4 | 7.4 |
| 14. BHP Billiton | 19.6 | 59.3 | 67. Devondale Murray Goulburn | 3.4 | 2.9 |
| 15. ExxonMobil Australia | 18.8 | 9.5 | 68. P Australia | 3.3 | 22.5 |
| 16. Perth Mint | 18.4 | 6.6 | 69. Orica | 3.2 | 5.7 |
| 17. Coca-Cola | 17.6 | 5.0 | 70. Boral | 3.2 | 4.4 |
| 18. Allianz Australia | 17.5 | 5.3 | 71. Metcash | 3.0 | 13.8 |
| 19. Ramsay Health Care | 17.4 | 7.4 | 72. NSW Health | 2.8 | 19.5 |
| 20. Commonwealth Bank | 17.0 | 45.3 | 73. Transport for NSW | 2.7 | 12.0 |
| 21. Viva Energy | 17.0 | 6.3 | 74. Spotless Group | 2.4 | 2.9 |
| 22. Daimler | 15.9 | 3.2 | 75. Caltex | 2.2 | 24.2 |
| 23. BUPA Australia | 15.7 | 6.2 | 76. Origin Energy | 2.0 | 11.9 |
| 24. Chevron Australia | 15.5 | 3.1 | 77. Dept. of Justice Corrective | | |
| 25. Westpac | 14.6 | 39.7 | Services NSW | 2.0 | 5.9 |
| 26. Medibank Private | 14.6 | 6.7 | 78. Victorian Dept. of Justice | | |
| 27. ANZ Banking Group | 14.0 | 36.4 | & Regulation | 1.2 | 5.3 |
| 28. Lendlease Group | 13.8 | 13.6 | 79. Public Transport Victoria | 0.8 | 4.1 |
| 29. Woodside | 13.8 | 9.2 | 80. Queensland Health | 0.4 | 15.2 |
| 30. WorleyParsons | 12.2 | 8.8 | 81. Sigma Pharmaceuticals | 0.0 | 3.2 |
| 31. Shell Energy Holdings | 12.0 | 6.4 | 82. Orora | -0.3 | 3.4 |
| 32. Crown Resorts | 12.0 | 3.5 | 83. API | -1.0 | 3.5 |
| 33. A P Eagers | 12.0 | 2.9 | 84. Broadspectrum | -3.2 | 3.8 |
| 34. WorkSafe Victoria | 11.6 | 3.6 | 85. Santos | -3.4 | 4.3 |
| 35. Sonic Healthcare | 11.4 | 4.2 | 86. Sims Metal Management | -4.2 | 6.4 |
| 36. NAB | 11.0 | 43.7 | 87. News Australia Holdings | -4.4 | 3.0 |
| 37. Automotive Holdings | 11.0 | 5.2 | 88. Lion Nathan National Foods | -4.8 | 4.8 |
| 38. Insurance Australia | 10.8 | 15.0 | 89. Queensland Treasury | | |
| 39. Alcoa Australia | 10.3 | 3.9 | Corporation | -5.8 | 8.2 |
| 40. Reserve Bank Australia | 10.0 | 8.6 | 90. Toyota Motor Corporation | -7.8 | 8.3 |
| 41. Incitec Pivot | 10.0 | 3.7 | 91. South32 | -8.0 | 6.5 |
| 42. Synergy | 9.6 | 3.2 | 92. BlueScope Steel | -10.6 | 8.6 |
| 43. AMP | 9.5 | 17.6 | 93. Virgin Australia | -11.8 | 4.8 |
| 44. CIMIC Group | 9.3 | 16.9 | 94. Newcrest Mining | -13.4 | 4.4 |
| 45. Wesfarmers | 9.0 | 62.8 | 95. Arrium Mining and Materials | -16.4 | 6.0 |
| 46. Macquarie Group | 8.6 | 12.2 | 96. Qantas | -16.5 | 15.9 |
| 47. SingTel Optus | 8.0 | 8.9 | 97. DOHS | -45.2 | 4.3 |
| 48. GrainCorp | 7.8 | 4.1 | 98. Foxtel | -51.6 | 3.2 |
| 49. Bendigo & Adelaide Bank | 7.8 | 3.3 | 99. GM Holden | -58.8 | 3.7 |
| 50. Australia Post | 7.6 | 6.4 | 100. Anglo American Australia | -65.0 | 3.3 |
| 51. Asciano | 7.6 | 3.8 | | | |
| 52. Downer EDI | 7.4 | 7.0 | Weighted Average/Total | 10.0 | 1070.0 |
| 53. CBH Group | 7.2 | 3.8 | | | |

SOURCE: IBISWORLD 01/05/2016

# The Best 100 Businesses

We now turn to the better news. Australia's Best 100 enterprises had a much smaller footprint, with combined revenues of $72 billion. Nevertheless, all are considered big enterprises, none being in the SME category of size. Four of them were in the Biggest 100 list (T-Corp, Apple, CSL and JB Hi-Fi). The relevant charts, comparable to the Big 100, are shown below. The contrast is striking, to say the least!

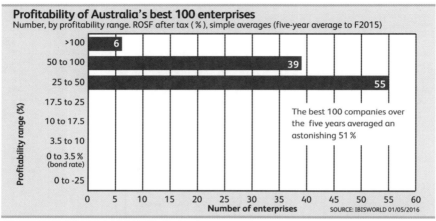

**Profitability of Australia's best 100 enterprises**
Number, by profitability range. ROSF after tax ( % ), simple averages (five-year average to F2015)

The best 100 companies over the five years averaged an astonishing 51 %

SOURCE: IBISWORLD 01/05/2016

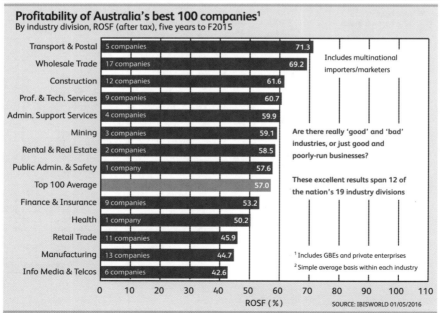

**Profitability of Australia's best 100 companies[1]**
By industry division, ROSF (after tax), five years to F2015

Includes multinational importers/marketers

Are there really 'good' and 'bad' industries, or just good and poorly-run businesses?

These excellent results span 12 of the nation's 19 industry divisions

[1] Includes GBEs and private enterprises
[2] Simple average basis within each industry

SOURCE: IBISWORLD 01/05/2016

It demonstrates so clearly, that there aren't really 'bad' industries to be in, just bad management.

The list of the Best 100 enterprises is provided below. All are in colour because all are at the top end of WBP.

## 100 Best Performing Australian Enterprises
Five years average ROSF, after tax ( % ), to 2015

| Enterprise | ROSF (%) | Revenue ($ million) | Enterprise | ROSF (%) | Revenue ($ million) |
|---|---|---|---|---|---|
| 1. Philip Morris | 189 | 950 | 51. OrotonGroup | 48 | 132 |
| 2. FedEx Australia | 120 | 229 | 52. LDC Enterprises Australia | 47 | 412 |
| 3. British American Tobacco | 107 | 2073 | 53. Colliers International | 46 | 311 |
| 4. Wood Group Australia | 104 | 561 | 54. Hyder Consulting | 46 | 104 |
| 5. AIRR | 101 | 298 | 55. Revlon Australia | 46 | 98 |
| 6. Jan De Nul (Australia) | 101 | 768 | 56. Grant Thornton Australia | 45 | 225 |
| 7. GSM Holding Company | 99 | 528 | 57. Monadelphous | 45 | 1874 |
| 8. Urbis | 97 | 79 | 58. Inchcape Australia | 45 | 2215 |
| 9. Hays Specialist Recruit. | 95 | 1517 | 59. Coca-Cola South Pacific | 44 | 145 |
| 10. Winslow Constructors | 91 | 331 | 60. Cover-More | 44 | 224 |
| 11. Hatch | 89 | 430 | 61. Mazda Australia | 44 | 2556 |
| 12. Philips Electronics | 86 | 383 | 62. UBS Holdings | 44 | 582 |
| 13. Dalrymple Bay Coal | 86 | 184 | 63. DuluxGroup | 43 | 1693 |
| 14. Schroder Investment | 85 | 188 | 64. Byrnecut Group | 43 | 606 |
| 15. Maurice Blackburn | 83 | 185 | 65. Hollard Australia Group | 43 | 250 |
| 16. Bakers Delight | 80 | 87 | 66. Masterton Group | 43 | 239 |
| 17. Norman Disney & Young | 80 | 73 | 67. Nestle | 42 | 2137 |
| 18. Metro Trains | 74 | 1303 | 68. Terry Shields Toyota | 42 | 167 |
| 19. Frasers Property Australia | 73 | 1142 | 69. Frucor Beverages | 42 | 212 |
| 20. ISGM | 72 | 451 | 70. Esri Australia | 41 | 75 |
| 21. Simonds Homes | 72 | 629 | 71. Boehringer Ingelheim | 41 | 356 |
| 22. Harry The Hirer | 71 | 72 | 72. Zara | 41 | 179 |
| 23. Dredging Internat. (Aust) | 68 | 796 | 73. Flinders Port | 41 | 201 |
| 24. TCorp | 67 | 4685 | 74. Kyocera | 41 | 97 |
| 25. AWX Group | 67 | 162 | 75. Reckon | 41 | 101 |
| 26. Interpublic Group | 66 | 260 | 76. QIC | 41 | 324 |
| 27. Schindler Lifts | 64 | 299 | 77. Australian Fleet Sales | 41 | 137 |
| 28. Novo Nordisk | 64 | 209 | 78. WorkPac | 40 | 633 |
| 29. L'Oreal Australia | 63 | 481 | 79. Nick Scali | 39 | 157 |
| 30. Tamawood | 60 | 95 | 80. GHD Group | 38 | 1573 |
| 31. Sunstate Cement | 59 | 137 | 81. Kane Constructions | 38 | 447 |
| 32. NSW DFSI | 58 | 1514 | 82. Interactive | 38 | 149 |
| 33. REALX Group | 56 | 212 | 83. Mars | 38 | 1392 |
| 34. Toshiba International | 55 | 98 | 84. Talent International | 37 | 329 |
| 35. Jaguar & Land Rover | 54 | 833 | 85. Metso | 37 | 401 |
| 36. Jardine Lloyd Thompson | 54 | 217 | 86. CSL | 37 | 7310 |
| 37. Hype DC | 53 | 94 | 87. Sensis | 37 | 864 |
| 38. Platinum Asset Management | 52 | 365 | 88. Alcatel-Lucent | 37 | 508 |
| 39. JB Hi-Fi | 52 | 3653 | 89. Green's Foods | 37 | 198 |
| 40. carsales.com | 52 | 316 | 90. REA Group | 36 | 558 |
| 41. Apple | 52 | 8003 | 91. Palladium Group | 36 | 388 |
| 42. Hassell | 52 | 100 | 92. Sydney Harbour Tunnel Co. | 36 | 130 |
| 43. Lorna Jane | 52 | 189 | 93. SMR Automotive Aust. | 36 | 133 |
| 44. Brighton Toyota/Lexus | 51 | 196 | 94. Penfold Motors Group | 36 | 304 |
| 45. Colgate-Palmolive | 51 | 538 | 95. J & P Richardson | 36 | 131 |
| 46. Specsavers | 50 | 654 | 96. Data#3 | 36 | 870 |
| 47. Garry Crick Auto Group | 50 | 70 | 97. Smith & Nephew | 36 | 101 |
| 48. Optiver Australia | 49 | 423 | 98. Omya Australia | 36 | 100 |
| 49. KONE Holdings (Australia) | 48 | 407 | 99. Ferrero Aust | 35 | 229 |
| 50. Cigweld | 48 | 94 | 100. Ainsworth Game Tech. | 35 | 270 |
| | | | Weighted Average/Total | 56 | 72000 |

SOURCE: IBISWORLD 01/05/2016

## So What?

The big end of town, by and large, doesn't display a lot of talent and competence in running big companies. Our Biggest 100 companies averaged a disappointing 10% ROSF over the five years to 2015. If the list was extended to the Biggest 1400 enterprises, the weighted average would drop to 6.5%, as shown below!

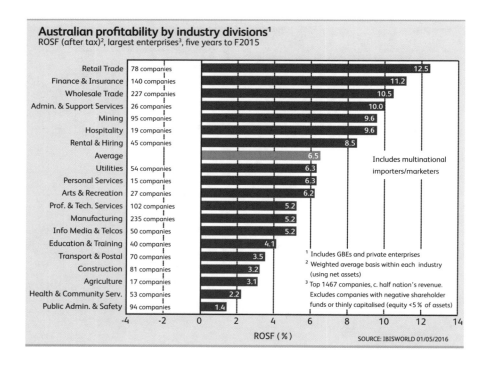

**Australian profitability by industry divisions[1]**
ROSF (after tax)[2], largest enterprises[3], five years to F2015

| Industry | Companies | ROSF (%) |
|---|---|---|
| Retail Trade | 78 companies | 12.5 |
| Finance & Insurance | 140 companies | 11.2 |
| Wholesale Trade | 227 companies | 10.5 |
| Admin. & Support Services | 26 companies | 10.0 |
| Mining | 95 companies | 9.6 |
| Hospitality | 19 companies | 9.6 |
| Rental & Hiring | 45 companies | 8.5 |
| Average | | 6.5 |
| Utilities | 54 companies | 6.3 |
| Personal Services | 15 companies | 6.3 |
| Arts & Recreation | 27 companies | 6.2 |
| Prof. & Tech. Services | 102 companies | 5.2 |
| Manufacturing | 235 companies | 5.2 |
| Info Media & Telcos | 50 companies | 5.2 |
| Education & Training | 40 companies | 4.1 |
| Transport & Postal | 70 companies | 3.5 |
| Construction | 81 companies | 3.2 |
| Agriculture | 17 companies | 3.1 |
| Health & Community Serv. | 53 companies | 2.2 |
| Public Admin. & Safety | 94 companies | 1.4 |

Includes multinational importers/marketers

[1] Includes GBEs and private enterprises
[2] Weighted average basis within each industry (using net assets)
[3] Top 1467 companies, c. half nation's revenue. Excludes companies with negative shareholder funds or thinly capitalised (equity <5% of assets)

ROSF (%)

SOURCE: IBISWORLD 01/05/2016

Australia has long lagged the USA and the UK (less so) in performance. The next chart (overleaf) shows the profitability of the *30 Largest Listeds* in the USA and Australia, showing the significant performance gap for the heavies in the respective stock exchanges (NYSE and ASX).

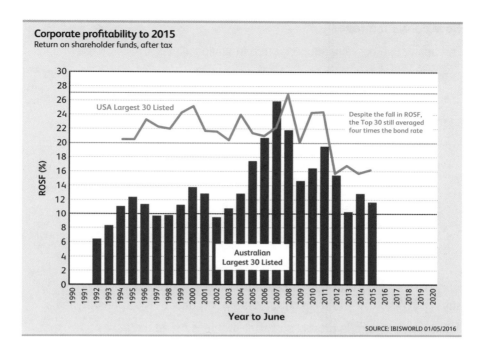

**Corporate profitability to 2015**
Return on shareholder funds, after tax

USA Largest 30 Listed

Despite the fall in ROSF, the Top 30 still averaged four times the bond rate

Australian Largest 30 Listed

ROSF (%)

Year to June

SOURCE: IBISWORLD 01/05/2016

Clearly, the only time our Top 30 Listeds achieved WBP was due to the serendipity of a mining boom. Interestingly, our stockmarket is dominated by mining and financial institutions, whereas the US stockmarkets is dominated by high-tech companies (IT, pharmaceuticals, etc.) with a lot less weight in mining and finance. That said, crooked behaviour by the Finance sector led to the USA's (and other countries') GFC in the mid-noughties. However, the much better results in the USA seem less to do with their industry mix than to do with their management.

In a separate IBISWorld monograph entitled ***Business Success***, we explain just what our Best 100 businesses do differently to the also-rans. The keys to success are listed and supported by statistics and analysis dating back to the 1970s.

## How do we improve?

Perhaps with a coordinated program that could include:

- Wider distribution of successful companies' *keys to success*;
- A rethink on Board structures, selection, abilities and priorities;
- Longer term goals for CEOs, and rewards accordingly;
- A rethink on the targets and curricula of our Business and MBA faculties;
- A reorientation of our business associations (AICD, Business Council, AIG, etc.) towards profitability not just conferences, compliance, consultations, fellowship and lobbying; and
- Strategic alliances between business institutes and universities (business/ MBA faculties).

The payback could be significant: why look for lower company taxes – say, 15-25% lower – to raise net profits by only about 15% at best, when a 100% improvement in pre-tax and after-profits is called for?

# Restoring Full Employment

*IBISWorld Newsletter* April 2016

nemployment can be soul destroying, especially for those responsible for a complete household's welfare. In the 20th century, governments finally took responsibility for those without a job. The dole was a term used to cover the work provided by state governments in the 1930s in the form of public works, and it provided some sustenance and dignity to the needy.

Over a decade later in 1945, the chiefly Labor Government formalised unemployment relief at the federal level. At around a fifth of the average wage or less, it was arguably all our taxes could afford in the 1940s and 1950s. It is higher today, but still just under a quarter.

Unemployment in Australia is cyclical but these cycles are not necessarily of equal length. The worst peaks have coincided with depressions in the 1840s, 1890s, 1930s and during the Federal Labor Government in the 1990s. The peaks averaged 50 years apart but actually ranged from 38 years to 61 years apart.

The last three peaks are shown in the chart below, occurring in 1894

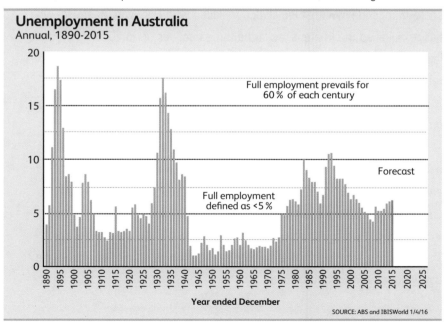

**Unemployment in Australia**
Annual, 1890-2015

Full employment prevails for 60 % of each century

Forecast

Full employment defined as <5 %

Year ended December

SOURCE: ABS and IBISWorld 1/4/16

(18.7%), 1932 (17.6%) and 1992 (almost 11%). The 1930s figure is often disputed, largely due to unemployment among union members, which was much higher than the overall labour force average. The worst depression and unemployment in the nation's history was not, as many claim, in the Great Depression of the 1930s. It was in the 15 year period from 1892 to 1906.

However, the longest and most disgraceful period of unemployment in our history was more recent, from 1977 to 2005: an almost three-decade long elongated depression.

Unlike previous depressions, the cause of the more recent unemployment cycle was due to bloody-mindedness by unions (opposing work sharing), businesses (working hours and other rigidities) and governments (binding IR regulations). So all three share the blame.

The current upsurge since 2009 has corresponded with the GFC but not with a recession in Australia; we haven't had one since 1992, nearly a quarter of a century ago. So what is the real cause of our current unemployment?

Clearly, the Work Choices legislation under the Howard Coalition Government worked, restoring full employment to the nation. But politics and scare-mongering saw that legislation replaced with Fair Work Australia, which has re-rigidified the IR arena, as in the three decades up to 2005. And that legislation is treated as a hot potato by the current Coalition government, which refuses to revisit and reform the legislation.

The US has restored full employment, arguably with overly-free labour force regulations. If so, where is the middle ground?

The good news is that we currently employ 49.0% of the nation's 24 million population. That remains close to our record-high level of several years ago, and way higher than the 40.0% of the 1960s when we had virtually no unemployment as the chart on the previous page shows.

However, the jobs are in vastly different places than 50 years ago. The next chart reminds us that service industries now dominate, as they do throughout the developed world.

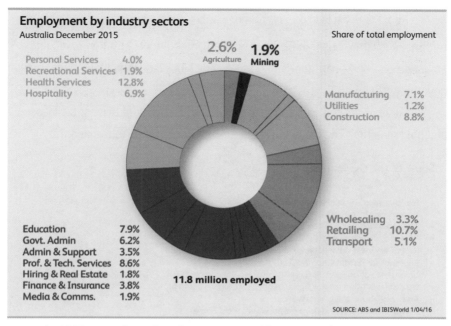

**Employment by industry sectors**
Australia December 2015

Share of total employment

| | |
|---|---|
| Personal Services | 4.0% |
| Recreational Services | 1.9% |
| Health Services | 12.8% |
| Hospitality | 6.9% |

2.6% Agriculture    **1.9% Mining**

| | |
|---|---|
| Manufacturing | 7.1% |
| Utilities | 1.2% |
| Construction | 8.8% |

| | |
|---|---|
| Wholesaling | 3.3% |
| Retailing | 10.7% |
| Transport | 5.1% |

| | |
|---|---|
| Education | 7.9% |
| Govt. Admin | 6.2% |
| Admin & Support | 3.5% |
| Prof. & Tech. Services | 8.6% |
| Hiring & Real Estate | 1.8% |
| Finance & Insurance | 3.8% |
| Media & Comms. | 1.9% |

**11.8 million employed**

SOURCE: ABS and IBISWorld 1/04/16

In 1960, manufacturing alone accounted for 30.0% of the jobs, but now makes up just 7.1%! But the encouraging news is that we are creating five times more jobs each year than we are losing, as seen in the next chart.

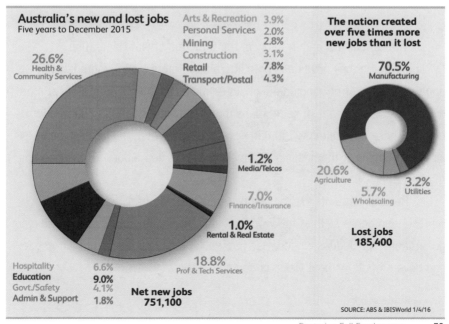

**Australia's new and lost jobs**
Five years to December 2015

| | |
|---|---|
| Arts & Recreation | 3.9% |
| Personal Services | 2.0% |
| Mining | 2.8% |
| Construction | 3.1% |
| Retail | 7.8% |
| Transport/Postal | 4.3% |

**The nation created over five times more new jobs than it lost**

26.6% Health & Community Services

70.5% Manufacturing

1.2% Media/Telcos

20.6% Agriculture    3.2% Utilities

7.0% Finance/Insurance

5.7% Wholesaling

1.0% Rental & Real Estate

**Lost jobs 185,400**

| | |
|---|---|
| Hospitality | 6.6% |
| **Education** | **9.0%** |
| Govt./Safety | 4.1% |
| Admin & Support | 1.8% |

18.8% Prof & Tech Services

**Net new jobs 751,100**

SOURCE: ABS & IBISWorld 1/4/16

So much for the doomsayers. We could create even more with overdue reforms across the board in IR, taxation, parliamentary constitution (inhibiting an undemocratic Senate that can permanently block legislation by the elected government) and other areas.

So what are the challenges to the vested interests of unions, businesses and governments? The following list is a controversial start to the debate.

---

**Some of the challenges**
For businesses, governments, unions and workers

- No 'bondage' by businesses, bosses or unions . . .
- . . . replaced by opportunity and empowerment
- The gradual demise of the concept of an 'employee'
- Rise of contractual relationships (a worker being a business)
- Rise of business ownership (workers owning a business)
- Payment for outputs, not inputs (hours of work)
- Emergence of advisers and mentors for worker contracts
- No discrimination on any basis (gender/race/age/religion etc)
- More part-time and casual work
- Partial or total working from home, where practicable
- More working seasons in a life
- New industries & occupations
- Working in a borderless world
- Knowledge worker concept
- Lifetime education & training
- Rising wages & salaries

SOURCE: IBISWORLD 01/04/16

---

The list will not bother many of the Gen Xers or Net Generation (Millennials), as they have been born into a freer, more global, more positive, opportunistic and free-ranging era in our unfolding economic progress. Far more entrepreneurs are in these generations than in any other period of our modern history. These days, almost 300,000 new businesses are created each year, albeit with many of them failing. But many initiators come back for a second or third attempt.

Resistance to necessary change tends to come from unions (now representing only a sixth of the workforce and declining), baby-boomer and older generations, ideologues, uninformed but well-intentioned clerics and do-gooders, and governments without vision or courage, or both.

Employment provides dignity and wealth that unemployment and the dole cannot match. Yes, we need relief for the unemployed, but not permanent crutches and the dreaded nanny state of some European nations.

We need to drive via the windscreen, not the rear vision mirror. The world is too promising to wring our hands or have inaction and silly ideologies that just don't cut it.

# National Leadership

*IBISWorld Newsletter* March 2016

Fifteen years into the new century, it is hard to find good leadership in many of the world's 230 nations. It's just as scarce among the 34 largely developed economies in the Organisation for Economic Co-operation and Development (OECD), including Australia. Yes, New Zealand, Switzerland, most of the Scandinavian countries and a handful of others make the cut, but most others don't, or – with new leadership – are yet to prove themselves.

By good leadership, we don't mean who's popular in the polls. History shows that popularity has nothing to do with good government. Heads of state and many ministers are often lacking in knowledge, vision, wisdom, courage and salesmanship to lead voters and economies. But they can still be popular.

Many far-sighted analysts are now even asking whether democracy can survive the 21st century with so many minorities demanding to be obeyed at the expense of the majority.

So what does a well-led nation need? The list below suggests the most important things.

### What a well-led nation needs

1. Safety (from external or internal threats, terrorism or anarchy)
2. Cohesive secular society (free of religious, ethnic, or any discrimination)
3. Democratic government (with compulsory voting?)
4. A mostly happy and caring society (with welfare for the needy)
5. A healthy, well-educated and increasingly cultured population
6. A proud, unique and fun-loving nation (but free of jingoism)
7. Continual reform (social, economic and political)
8. Full employment (unemployment 5% or less)
9. Economic growth and rising standard of living (2% pa or more)
10. Low inflation (less than 3%)
11. Fair interest rates (to depositors and borrowers alike, around 5% real)
12. Productivity growth (around 2% pa)
13. A strong exchange rate
14. Balanced government budgets (low national debt, less than 35% of GDP)
15. A positive current account with the world (paying our own way)

SOURCE: IBISWORLD 01/03/16

The world had its last recession in 2009, three generations and 63 years after the previous one in 1946. It would have been a depression if not for massive ongoing deficit spending across the world – the equivalent of fiscal morphine. This spending has drugged populations into a false sense of security and slowed growth to almost a standstill in many parts of the world, including the EU, Japan and the USA. Asia, with over 6% gross domestic product (GDP) growth, has accounted for half of the world's GDP growth for the past eight years or so, with the OECD group limping on with less than 2% per annum, or half its long-term average of 3.5%.

Australia gets a lot of the above right – after all, we are in the world's Top 10 Standard of Living (GDP/capita) countries, and we have five of the world's Top 10 most liveable cities.

But the nation has been reform-aversive for most of this century, partly a result of the lack of a wake-up call – such as a recession – since 1992. So half the nation's workforce of 11.8 million has never experienced such a shock; they weren't in the workforce then. Clearly the boiling-frog syndrome is at work in its usual insidious way. With or without a recession, various governments should have given us that wake-up call.

So what are the issues that our Federal Government should be addressing, and are they doing so? The list below suggests the main issues.

**Our Federal Government: a to-do list**
(And are they being adressed?)

| | |
|---|---|
| 1. National literacy and perspective: economic; financial; and digital age | No |
| 2. Senate reform: unrepresentative and bills-rejection problems | No |
| 3. Balanced budgets: the first rule of good government | No |
| 4. Tax reform: that includes GST and shifts taxes to spending | No |
| 5. IR reform: that understands work and workers in the New Age | No |
| 6. Innovation: IP and productivity, and how to get them | No |
| 7. Fully embrace the digital era: for international competitiveness | No |
| 8. Privatisation: of low-productivity government activities | No |
| 9. Long-range vision: especially our role in the Asia Pacific region | Yes/No |
| 10. Reduce subsidies going to yesterday's industries that won't survive | Yes/No |
| 11. Rational energy policy, that includes carbon, nuclear power | Yes/No |
| 12. Developing the top part of our continent (especially top 1/3) | Yes/No |

SOURCE: IBISWORLD 01/03/16

The number of 'no' actions is not just regrettable, but also harmful for the medium to longer term. Over the longer term, this inaction will cause Australia to lag well behind our neighbours in economic terms.

The nation's current PM came to power making promises in many of these areas, and emphasising that reforms required more perspective and explanation given to the voters – plus compelling salesmanship – so that voters can make more rational decisions. Indeed, national literacy and perspective are sadly lacking on matters such as how a modern economy functions, taxation perspectives (historical and global), financial and investment variables, and the digital age. There are factions between members of parliament, divisive and combative politics, and at times shallow if not shock-jock journalism.

Effective government can be stymied by a lack of democracy in our upper house – the Senate – which has become the de facto ruling house. With 12 senators per state, regardless of electoral size, and the legal aggregation of votes by independents and narrow-interest parties to gain many of these seats, the term 'unrepresentative swill', coined by Paul Keating, seems very apt.

And, unlike the UK Westminster system, our upper house can reject bills ad infinitum, whereas in Britain the upper house can only delay them. The democratically elected House of Representatives is no longer the governing body. It is the Senate – the so-called house of review – with the power.

One possible reform after another is being shelved or emasculated, as 2016 heads towards a federal election later in the year. These include tax reform, labour market reform and parliamentary reform. Our digital age opportunities are constrained by having one of the developed world's slowest and least rolled-out fast-broadband networks. There is minimal coverage of the nation's 2.1 million businesses and 9.6 million dwellings. Many, if not most, members of parliament are ignorant of the criticality of this problem and do not realise the resulting impairment of innovation and productivity in the economy.

The nation needs great leadership, a not-so-common commodity in Australia's short modern history of around 220 years.

This article began with a list of what a well-led and well-run nation needs. So, which heads of government have passed these tests over the centuries? Only one in four, as it turns out, not including laudable reformers or others who got a lot, but not most of it, right. The following list identifies the 19 leaders/ statesmen and some key reformers. It should be noted that in the interval period between the formation of sovereign states and federation, the analysis had to assess key state premiers, rather than governors in the first half of the 19th century and the arrival of PMs in the 20th century.

## Australia's best leaders

Those who made Australia very prosperous.
Those who were change agents and reformers.

| # | Name | Title | # | Name | Title |
|---|------|-------|---|------|-------|
| 1. | Cptn. Arthur Phillip | (Govnr.) | | Edmund Barton | (PM) |
| 2. | Cptn. Philip King | (Govnr.) | 12. | Alfred Deakin | (PM) |
| 3. | Maj. Gen. Macquarie | (Govnr.) | 13. | Andrew Fisher | (PM) |
| 4. | Maj. Gen. R. Darling | (Govnr.) | 14. | William Hughes | (PM) |
| 5. | Maj. Gen. Bourke | (Govnr.) | | Joseph Lyons | (PM) |
| 6. | Sir Charles Fitz Roy | (Govnr.) | 15. | Robert Menzies | (PM) |
| 7. | Sir William Denison | (Govnr.) | 16. | John Curtin | (PM) |
| 8. | Sir J McCulloch | (Prem. Vic.) | 17. | J. Ben Chifley | (PM) |
| | Sir Henry Parkes | (Prem. NSW) | 18. | John Gorton | (PM) |
| 9. | James Service | (Prem. Vic.) | | Gough Whitlam | (PM) |
| 10. | George Reid | (Prem. NSW) | | Robert Hawke | (PM) |
| 11. | Sir George Turner | (Prem. Vic.) | 19. | John Howard | (PM) |

SOURCE: IBISWORLD 01/03/16

Such a list will always spark controversy because the facts may be inconvenient or distasteful. Politics is often more emotional than rational and we find the same when we are talking religion or sport.

Good reformers such as Hawke and Keating are left off the list because of massive unemployment, chronic deficit spending, massive national debt build-up, record-high mortgage interest rates and other negatives on the economy and households during that 13 year period. Despite all the great work, the core elements of a well-run economy were not there for the 13 years.

Interestingly, there were as many Labor PMs as Conservative PMs on the best leaders list for the 20th century – three and a half each. How come the 'half', it may well be asked! Because William (Billy) Hughes was PM at one time for Labor and at another time for the National Party (conservative).

An IBISWorld study of the 76 leaders up to Tony Abbott revealed that political party ideology and platforms may have influenced voters and the appointment of PMs but were irrelevant to great leadership. Success was not built on hyperbole, jingoism and rhetoric. Pragmatism and action always spoke louder than words.

So what were the distinguishing characteristics of the 19 best leaders in our history? The next list details the dozen factors that were common in over 85% of the leaders.

### Characteristics of successful heads of state

1. They were mostly elected in the last one-sixth of their then life expectancy at birth (a legacy to be left rather than self-aggrandisement)
2. They were mostly civics, none were idealists or ideologues
3. They were mostly conservatives using platforms to win office, then running the country pragmatically
4. They had a middle or working class background (easier to relate to)
5. They were mostly professionals or tradesmen rather than businessmen
6. They were mostly born in second-string states (something to prove?)
7. Most had been blooded (militarily or psychologically beforehand)
8. They were tough, resolute and even ruthless when necessary, but often lonely, aloof, moody and unsure
9. They had a loyal aide who supported the leader
10. They fashioned the economy rather than managed it
11. They ran balanced budgets, eschewing debt build-up
12. They were all males (but unlikely in the 21st century), and they were more likely to be Librans, Virgos or Taureans, followed by Capricorns and Leos: go figure!

SOURCE: IBISWORLD 01/03/16

These characteristics are not immutable and there were some exceptions with the best leaders. Not all the great leaders gave a tick to every single one of the points above. And, furthermore, a nation can have good and average leaders that are not great statesmen, but were adequate.

Do we have a leader with these success attributes, and are there other candidates in the major political camps? Time will tell. What we do know is that the last three PMs did not make the list of great statesmen, or even a good or average list. However, with or without a great leader at present, there are things we can be happy with, as the final exhibit shows.

**Why Australia can still smile in 2016**
But not be complacent

- We have one of the highest standards of living in the world
- We have the world's most livable city (Melbourne)
- And four others in the Top 10; how good is that!
- We are a confident nation (Consumer Sentiment)
- We are part of the world's fastest growing region: the Asia Pacific
- Our population growth is faster than the world's 1.3% pa
- We have virtually no serious racial tensions or terrorism
- Our unemployment, while not 'full', is among the OECD's lowest
- Our national debt is the lowest in the OECD as a percentage of GDP
- We are the third lowest taxed nation among the OECD rich countries
- Our deficits are chronic but low within the OECD, and fixable
- Our interest rates are low

SOURCE: IBISWORLD 01/03/16

But only for the time being. Let's make sure we're not only staying in the race, but that we're right up there with the leaders. And keep an ear out for those wake-up calls.

# Taxation Reform: Is Canberra Serious?

*Cuffelinks Newsletter* March 2016

The Roman emperor Nero, apocryphally, fiddled while Rome burned in 64 AD.

Few politicians in modern times can play a violin or fiddle, but they are very good at rhetoric, filibustering and backflipping. And this explains why in Australia they consistently score so low on the Roy Morgan ethics and honesty ladder: indeed, below 15 points out of a hundred, sitting with union leaders, but above drug dealers, car salesmen and realtors. If that is any consolation.

The wasted tax enquiries and summits of recent years testify to the insincerity or lack of courage of governments since the Howard/Costello era.

Facts have rarely been put on the table for the voting population to get perspective, either historical or international. Vested interests, as usual, are at it as hard as they can muster support for their rent-seeking, bleeding-heart platforms or political opportunism.

Voters should be advised or reminded that we are living beyond our means, and need to raise taxes – or cut welfare and support (political suicide) – to balance our budgets and arrest the growing national debt being left to our children. The public deserves perspective.

## So, what are the realities?

The first chart (overleaf) reveals that government at all three levels raised $555 billion in revenue in 2015, just over a third of the nation's gross domestic product (GDP). The vast majority of it is via taxes, supplemented by income from government business enterprises (GBEs) and borrowings for the deficit.

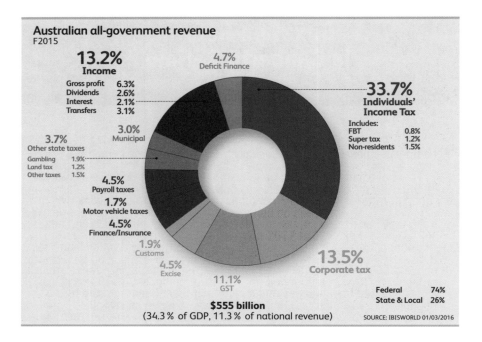

**Australian all-government revenue**
F2015

13.2%
Income

| | |
|---|---|
| Gross profit | 6.3% |
| Dividends | 2.6% |
| Interest | 2.1% |
| Transfers | 3.1% |

4.7%
Deficit Finance

33.7%
Individuals'
Income Tax

Includes:
| | |
|---|---|
| FBT | 0.8% |
| Super tax | 1.2% |
| Non-residents | 1.5% |

3.0%
Municipal

3.7%
Other state taxes

| | |
|---|---|
| Gambling | 1.9% |
| Land tax | 1.2% |
| Other taxes | 1.5% |

4.5%
Payroll taxes

1.7%
Motor vehicle taxes

4.5%
Finance/Insurance

1.9%
Customs

4.5%
Excise

11.1%
GST

13.5%
Corporate tax

| | |
|---|---|
| Federal | 74% |
| State & Local | 26% |

**$555 billion**
(34.3 % of GDP, 11.3 % of national revenue)

SOURCE: IBISWORLD 01/03/2016

It is nearly three times the share of GDP when the nation federated in 1901; but then, and for decades later, helping the less fortunate was a case of charity and family or tribal support. There was no national defence force; no pensions for the olds; no unemployment relief; no free education; little health care; no support for industries; nor many other support services which we take for granted – and would want to keep – today.

If anything, we could be regarded as a bit mean-spirited with a current level of taxation at 27.7% of GDP in 2015. This compares with over 30% not so long ago, and is far below the Organisation for Economic Co-operation and Development (OECD) average of 35% of GDP; but not as lavish as many so-called nanny-states at over 40%.

The mischievous, self-serving and fallacious argument about the damage done by an increasing in the GST and removing current exemptions on food, education and health to fixed-and low-income earners is scaremongering.

It ignores the accompanying protection to such vulnerable households that would be given by such legislation: Governments are loath to commit electoral suicide when it comes to taxation reform, so pensioners and other disadvantaged individuals and households would be largely compensated.

So, let's turn to some of the myths and lies about our current taxation system.

## Myth Number 1: We are highly taxed already

No, we are certainly not taxed highly by international standards, as seen in the second chart (below); and not by historical standards.

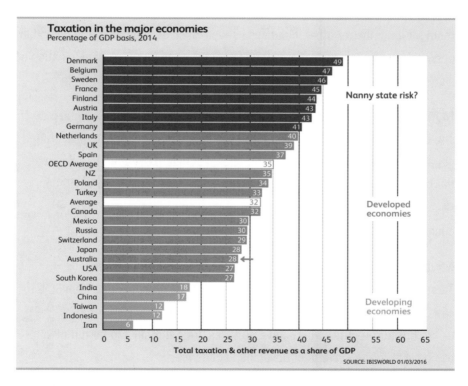

Let's put to rest the suggestion that we are highly taxed or overtaxed once and for all.

## Myth Number 2: Raising the GST is regressive

We are the lowest GST nation in the developed world at an effective average rate of 4.5% on goods and services, given the aforementioned exemptions. This compares with an effective average rate of 14% in the OECD; over three times our rate. It is hardly an unprecedented or risky step to raise the level as a way of balancing our budget.

Leaving the nominal rate at 10% but removing exemptions from the present regime would in itself lead to a balanced budget, provide room for compensation of the low-and fixed-income sectors of our population, and allow for adjustment to the tax thresholds arising from bracket-creep.

Raising the level to 12.5%, again without exemptions, would create room for a number of other initiatives as well, such as substantive reduction in personal income tax scales, reduction in corporate tax levels and elimination of some state taxes (e.g. stamp duties, payroll tax). Doable, one would think.

## Myth Number 3: Our payroll taxes are a disincentive to employ more staff

There is always talk of getting rid of payroll taxes, they being one of the bêtes noires of business. However, by international standards, we are low down the ladder of those that have labour taxes. Even if we lump superannuation payments (although they are not a tax, like social security taxes in other countries) into labour taxes, we are just over half the OECD average.

## Myth Number 4: Our corporate rate of tax is uncompetitive

There has been a more recent push to lower our corporate tax rate from 30% to, say, 25% (and lower the SME tax rate of 28.5% as well).

But the Australian corporate tax rates are not really too far out of kilter, being close to the average of developed economies.

There is a case to lower the tax rate if it would lead to higher investment from retained profits, thereby creating growth and productivity in the economy. A 27.5% rate would be a good start.

## Myth Number 5: The rich don't pay enough taxes

One of the few ugly genes in the Australian ethos is envy and covetousness, in stark contrast to the aspirational genes in the USA. Fairness and equanimity is one thing – and we are good at those things, by and large – but pulling down the 'tall poppies' is just plain silly.

The rich and well-off 40% of Australian households, do pay the vast bulk of all taxes anyway; a stonking 87%! Some 60% of households pay less than 13% of all taxes. So, there is a lot of humbug and politicking in the area of who is copping the tax load. As usual, facts ruin a good story – or lie.

That said, bracket-creep in the individual income tax regime – the automatic follow-on from rising wages and inflation – is an issue that governments must, and do, address from time to time.

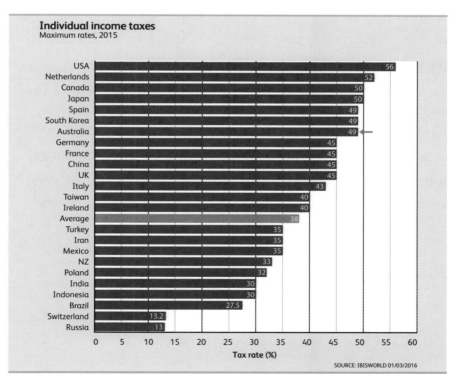

**Individual income taxes**
Maximum rates, 2015

SOURCE: IBISWORLD 01/03/2016

Our maximum individual income tax rate sits uncomfortably near the top of the international ladder as seen in the previous chart, so this and other threshold rates do need addressing as part of a reform package. The Treasurer is addressing this issue in the Government's deliberations. We are taxing our citizens – rich and middle class alike – too highly. We should be lowering these direct taxes and replacing them with higher *indirect* taxes, especially the GST. The rich and well-off will pay much more of this GST as a result anyway, compared with the lower-income households.

## After all this, what should we do?

We are blessed with a very low national debt in 2016 that acts as a fiscal safeguard to our economy, but we need tax reform nevertheless. We are living beyond our means, primarily by not raising enough taxes by historical or international standards to cover spending, although that is not wildly out of control.

To try and save our way into balanced budgets is regressive, and unachievable anyway. We would lose essential services by 21st century standards, and equanimity in the community.

We should alter the mix of taxes in favour of the *indirect* (wealth spending) taxes to encourage savings, investment and productivity. The GST should be increased. Income taxes should be lowered. And the potentially disadvantaged poor and fixed-income earners need to be compensated at the same time. These measures are all doable, with vision, courage and salesmanship.

# We Always Need Innovation, but What, Where and How?

*IBISWorld Newsletter* February 2016

N ations need innovation to grow, improve efficiency, and raise their standard of living and happiness. But innovation is a catch-all term with many facets.

We often think of innovation as being research and development (R&D) based, and in goods industries such as manufacturing, mining and agriculture. This is misleading. Most innovation is not necessarily a formally R&D-based activity, and is certainly not centred on goods industries nowadays.

The first chart reminds us of the economy we have going into 2016 — one increasingly dominated by service industries (72%). This is the case across the Organisation for Economic Co-operation and Development (OECD) group of developed countries, which account for the vast majority of the world's gross domestic product (GDP) in 2016.

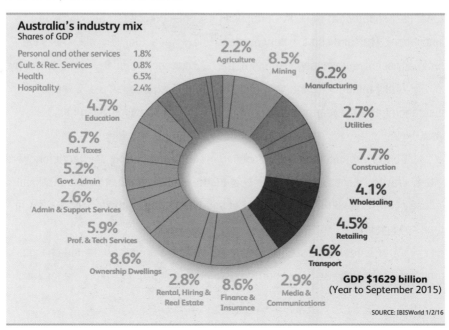

**Australia's industry mix**
Shares of GDP

| | |
|---|---|
| Personal and other services | 1.8% |
| Cult. & Rec. Services | 0.8% |
| Health | 6.5% |
| Hospitality | 2.4% |

2.2% Agriculture
8.5% Mining
6.2% Manufacturing
4.7% Education
2.7% Utilities
6.7% Ind. Taxes
7.7% Construction
5.2% Govt. Admin
4.1% Wholesaling
2.6% Admin & Support Services
4.5% Retailing
5.9% Prof. & Tech Services
4.6% Transport
8.6% Ownership Dwellings
2.8% Rental, Hiring & Real Estate
8.6% Finance & Insurance
2.9% Media & Communications

**GDP $1629 billion**
(Year to September 2015)

SOURCE: IBISWorld 1/2/16

The 19 industries on the chart (previous page) contain 509 classes of industry with an average revenue this financial year of $10 billion. Yet the range is diverse in both type and revenue, including: Pesticide Manufacturing ($1.1 billion); Commercial Laundries, and Holiday Houses, Flats and Hostels (each $1.2 billion); Internet Publishing and Broardcasting ($1.7 billion); Water Supply ($11.2 billion); Insurance Brokerage ($12.2 billion); Beef Cattle Farming ($12.6 billion); Computer System Design Services ($47.1 billion); General Hospitals ($62.1 billion); Supermarkets and Grocery Stores ($88.1 billion); and Superannuation Funds at a whopping $278.0 billion.

Growth rates over the next five years, averaging around 3.0% per annum, range from 27.5% per annum increases (Self-Managed Superannuation Funds) to 28.0% declines (Motor Vehicle Manufacturing) across the 509 industry classes.

These classes run in strongly defined cycles that average 40-45 years in length, once established as an industry. The second chart (top overleaf) shows the normal evolution and demise of an industry lifecycle, with all its phases and two scary periods, being the 'horror zone' (mature, over-supply period) and the 'terror zone' (last shootout at the O.K. Corral and onset of a completely new cycle of innovation). The third chart (below overleaf) shows an actual lifecycle, in this case for Pharmacies representing just one of the 509 classes of industry in the economy.

A tiny minority have longer and shorter cycles: for example, General Insurance has a 50-year cycle, and Wine and Brandy Manufacturing has a 25-year cycle.

Contrary to common belief, industry cycles aren't getting shorter or longer – they stay roughly the same length over centuries. Only product cycles within an industry class can sometimes be short or shortening. For example, Moore's law in the IT chip industry.

When a new cycle starts, there are always five areas of profound change: products, technology and/or systems, customer profiles and markets, geographic

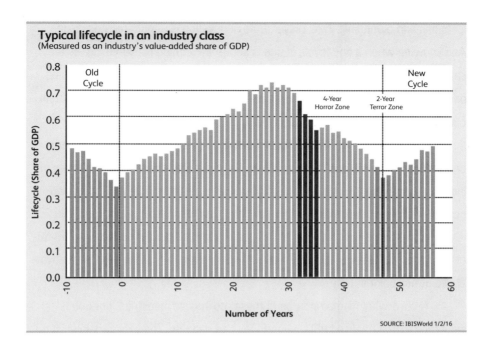

## Typical lifecycle in an industry class
(Measured as an industry's value-added share of GDP)

Old Cycle

New Cycle

4-Year Horror Zone

2-Year Terror Zone

Lifecycle (Share of GDP)

Number of Years

SOURCE: IBISWorld 1/2/16

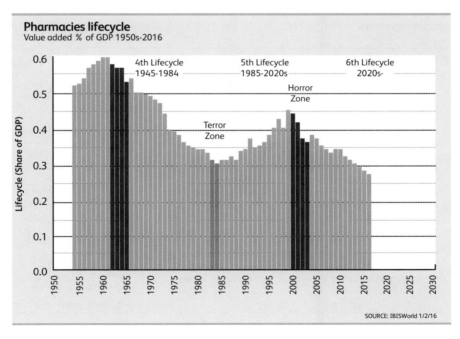

## Pharmacies lifecycle
Value added % of GDP 1950s-2016

4th Lifecycle 1945-1984

5th Lifecycle 1985-2020s

6th Lifecycle 2020s-

Horror Zone

Terror Zone

Lifecycle (Share of GDP)

SOURCE: IBISWorld 1/2/16

locations and ownership (new players). So, innovation is a multi-faceted issue. And knowing when a new cycle is due is important. Timing is everything, as they say. Often innovation is too early or too late in a cycle, and even picking the best new systems and technology – out of many competing options – can be a lottery. Economies have graveyards of ideas that didn't make the cut.

As said, major innovation takes place at the beginning of a new industry, or during a rebirth into another new cycle. So, given that there are 509 classes of industry with average cycle lengths of 40-45 years, there will be around a dozen new major innovations taking place every year. But, of course, given that such revolutions emerge over a period of five years or more, it could be said that 50-60 of the nation's classes of industry – a tenth of all of them – are in their innovative phase at any point in time.

An overwhelming proportion of these are service industries, not goods industries with formalised R&D, laboratories and gadgets. The exhibit below lists the newest and/or fastest growing industries in Australia's new age – mostly service industries.

---

**Fastest-growing industry themes**
New Age, 1965-2040s

- **ICT & Fast Broadband** – the New Age all-pervasive utility.
- **Knowledge Industries** – databases and multi-media services.
- **Business Services** – outsourcing non-core functions.
- **Financial Services** – outsourcing of transactions/investment.
- **Property Services** – outsourcing ownership, facilities management.
- **Health** – outsourcing home doctoring.
- **Education** – outsourcing pre-school, plus universities.
- **Personal & Household Services** – outsourcing chores.
- **Hospitality & Tourism** – outsourcing the kitchen and travel.
- **Recreation & Cultural Services** – outsourcing leisure.
- **Mining** – energy minerals (oil, gas, coal, uranium).
- **Construction** – cyclical, but growing importance of civil work.
- **Transport** – cyclical, but growth in road, air, pipeline and F/F.
- **Agribusiness in the North** – Asia's food security demand pull.
- **Biotechnology & Nanotechnology** – New Age technologies.
- **Environmental Services** – testing, assessment, amelioration.

SOURCE: IBISWORLD 01/02/16

---

Our exports of tourism and other services will easily outstrip mining exports by the end of the next decade; so what innovation is taking place in this potential goldmine? Are we outsourcing non-core business functions and household chores fast enough and being innovative in their supply back to the users?

The nation has revenue well over $1 trillion and employment of over three million these days, in the form of new age household and business services, spread over 80 new classes of industry since the mid-1960s and over a hundred more reborn classes of industry. These required innovation of the sort we see in facilities management services, IT outsourcing, and household services as provided by the likes of Jim's and VIP. Add new health services, add new financial, professional and technical services, and add new hospitality and entertainment services. These and other new services point to where innovation will occur.

That said, we cannot write off the minority goods sector industries when it comes to innovation. We do have over 1,000 advanced manufacturing businesses competing worldwide, even though they account for less than 1% of our GDP. Mining hasn't finished its volume growth yet, even if prices may have. And the food-security issue in Asia suggests we have a lot of innovation to do in agriculture to tap into this other goldmine too, as this exciting and prospective century unfolds.

All industries – be they goods- or services-based – benefit from pervasive utilities that aid their progress, growth, innovation and productivity. Transport was such a utility in the Agrarian Age, electricity in the Industrial Age, and ICT in our current age of services-based industries. This is expected to last until the middle of this century.

The recent Stage 2 of the ICT utility began in 2007 – in the form of the digital age of fast broadband, advanced software and analytics – and is breathtaking in its innovating assistance to new and long-standing industries alike. It is termed the digital-disruption era. Interestingly, this year, our ICT utility will have revenue just under $140 billion, but represent a mere 2.7% of the nation's revenue of over $5 trillion. Such is the leverage and innovative power of this modern utility.

All the more reason to have high-speed broadband (100MB/s to 1000MB/s) to every one of our 2.1 million businesses and 9.6 million homes. We are nowhere near this new world standard – we are not even in the top 25 nations, and won't be this side of the next decade. But it is one of the preconditions to being serious about innovation and productivity.

Our new PM is right: we do have an innovation challenge. Without innovation, companies, industries and economies stagnate. Productivity stalls, new industries fail to take off, growth rates fall, and standards of living level out and decline. This scenario is occurring across much of the developed world, including the EU, Japan and even the USA. And, to an extent, here in Australia, where we can least afford it as a member of the dynamic Asian region.

The current global economic malaise is rightly attributed to the GFC from late-2008 onwards, occasioned by greed, debt, deficits and financial skullduggery. Of course, these evils were present some years before the inevitable financial collapses took place, and have not yet all gone away. Innovation is not independent of fiscal impropriety or a badly managed economy. As the old saying goes: when you are up to your knees in alligators, it is hard to remember your original plan was to drain the swamp.

So innovation and productivity will be impeded in Australia if distractions aren't dealt with through IR reform (made more urgent by union corruption), taxation reform, balancing government budgets, a faster and higher speed broadband rollout, and reforming parliament to overcome the reform-stymieing actions of our unrepresentative and undemocratic Senate.

Our economic growth is running at almost a percentage point below our long term average of 3.5% per annum, and our productivity growth is half the long-term average of 1.7% per annum. It isn't much consolation to know that the EU and Japan are in far worse and perilous circumstances. Nevertheless, our electorate has been misled, frightened and confused by bad and/or incompetent governments for too long. There is a need to give people facts and perspective, but also to let people know the consequences of inaction. The endpoint of course is countries like Greece, Spain, Brazil and dozens of others – crippled by debt, massive unemployment and incompetence, if not endemic corruption.

A reform pathway is the one chosen by the current government – energised by a likely overwhelming endorsement at the coming election this year. We certainly need it to get out of our economic doldrums.

The rewards can be staggering if we get it right.

# What Australia is Worth

*IBISWorld Newsletter* December 2015

Australia's total resources in mid-2015 were estimated to be worth $13.5 trillion, over eight times our gross domestic product (GDP) in 2014-15. After allowing for foreign liabilities of $3.0 trillion, our net assets were $10.5 trillion, or around $1.1 million per household. The land, natural resources and built environment dominate this balance sheet as the first chart shows, with just under a quarter made up of financial assets (15.4%), IP, equipment, inventories and household durables.

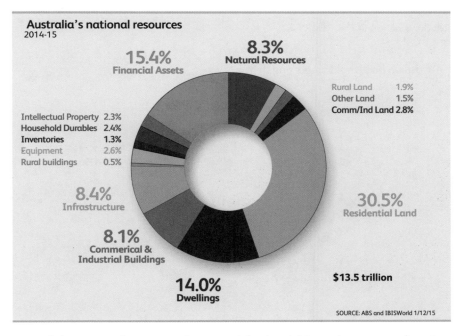

**Australia's national resources**
2014-15

- 15.4% Financial Assets
- 8.3% Natural Resources
- Rural Land 1.9%
- Other Land 1.5%
- Comm/Ind Land 2.8%
- Intellectual Property 2.3%
- Household Durables 2.4%
- Inventories 1.3%
- Equipment 2.6%
- Rural buildings 0.5%
- 8.4% Infrastructure
- 8.1% Commerical & Industrial Buildings
- 14.0% Dwellings
- 30.5% Residential Land
- $13.5 trillion

SOURCE: ABS and IBISWorld 1/12/15

It is encouraging to note that our net foreign debt was less-concerning at a manageable $906 billion after allowing for our foreign assets of over $2.0 trillion.

Whilst purely academic, it is interesting to consider what a foreign country might pay for Australia, if only because countries – or parts of them – have been sold in the past. The USA paid $US 240.0 million (in today's terms) for the

Louisiana Purchase of 2.1 million square kilometres (28.0% of Australia's land mass) from France in 1803; and a similar amount for Alaska (20.0% of Australia's land mass) from Russia in 1867. Those acquisitions, nearly half of Australia's land mass, were acquired for under $US 500 million in today's terms: a steal, as they say. Australia wouldn't go for that cheap; try $50 trillion, so each family could retire with over $5 million each.

But don't float the idea, because any of several nations could afford that, and would come running with a chequebook – with the risk a lot of Australians might say yes!

The assets and net worth of households follows a similar break-up to the nation, as seen in the next chart.

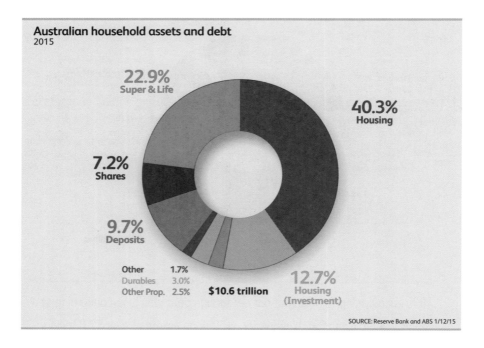

**Australian household assets and debt**
2015

22.9%
Super & Life

40.3%
Housing

7.2%
Shares

9.7%
Deposits

Other 1.7%
Durables 3.0%
Other Prop. 2.5%

**$10.6 trillion**

12.7%
Housing
(Investment)

SOURCE: Reserve Bank and ABS 1/12/15

However, in this case the financial assets are more significant; even more so when the net assets, or net worth of households, are broken up – as the next chart shows.

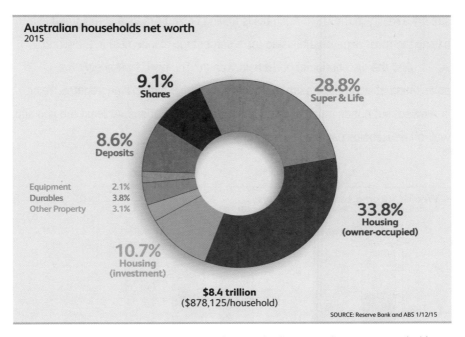

**Australian households net worth**
2015

**9.1%** Shares

**28.8%** Super & Life

**8.6%** Deposits

Equipment 2.1%
Durables 3.8%
Other Property 3.1%

**33.8%** Housing (owner-occupied)

**10.7%** Housing (investment)

**$8.4 trillion** ($878,125/household)

SOURCE: Reserve Bank and ABS 1/12/15

Indeed, it is the financial assets that are in the ascendancy as revealed in the next chart. The dominance of financial assets over housing and other assets is

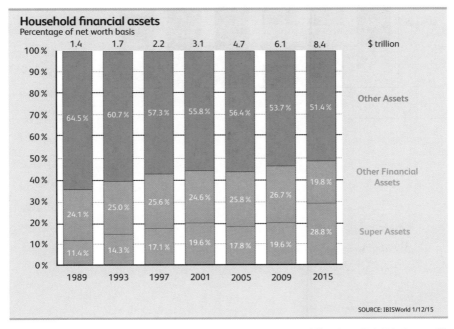

**Household financial assets**
Percentage of net worth basis

| | 1.4 | 1.7 | 2.2 | 3.1 | 4.7 | 6.1 | 8.4 | $ trillion |

Other Assets: 64.5%, 60.7%, 57.3%, 55.8%, 56.4%, 53.7%, 51.4%

Other Financial Assets: 19.8%

Super Assets: 24.1%, 25.0%, 25.6%, 24.6%, 25.8%, 26.7%, 28.8%

11.4%, 14.3%, 17.1%, 19.6%, 17.8%, 19.6%

1989 1993 1997 2001 2005 2009 2015

SOURCE: IBISWorld 1/12/15

already a reality in the USA. Australia is trailing behind America in this trend due to having the most expensive housing (as a percentage of incomes) in the world.

And the distribution of household wealth? The final chart shows the polarisation of incomes, wealth (net worth) and other financial aggregates. Yes it is skewed, but not as much as many other developed nations. At least the rich and well-off households pay the lion's share of the taxes.

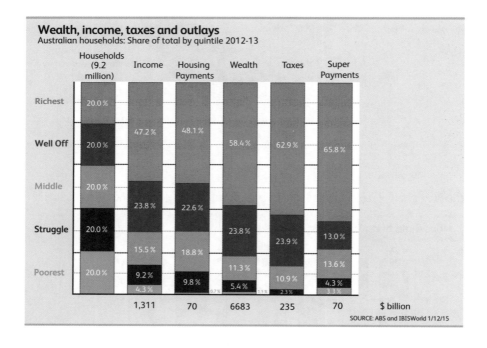

**Wealth, income, taxes and outlays**
Australian households: Share of total by quintile 2012-13

SOURCE: ABS and IBISWorld 1/12/15

# Knowing Where We Stand in Our Region

*IBISWorld Newsletter* September 2015

We need to develop more perspective and vision regarding the world outside our own country – a fast-emerging borderless world. Thanks to many developments over the past half century, we have more exposure to trade, investment, jobs, people movements and especially information. This represents a threat to some and an opportunity to others.

Most countries throughout the world sought a more peaceful coexistence after the two world wars, especially in Europe via the formation of the EU. But given the conflict in the Asia-Pacific in World War II, our neighbors in the region also sought a more peaceful world. APEC – a Hawke initiative in the 1980s – was a good start on this journey.

Since then, the freer movement of people through immigration and tourism has helped to create a better appreciation of different nations, their standards of living, their cultures, religions and politics.

The move to regional cooperation via defence pacts, free trade agreements and freer capital flows has been particularly beneficial to business and, therefore, economic growth.

All this makes it important to know where we stand in our region as this tumultuous century unfolds. Relative economic clout is a useful start. The first chart reveals the relative importance of the more than 25 nations in our region, breaking down gross domestic product (GDP) of some US$30 trillion in purchasing power parity (PPP) terms in 2015-16.

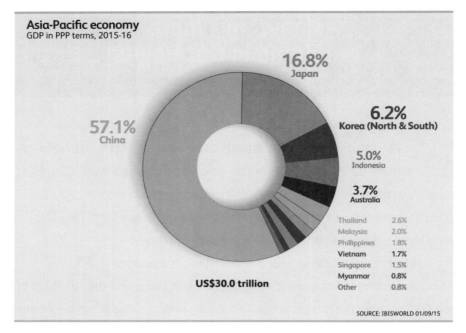

**Asia-Pacific economy**
GDP in PPP terms, 2015-16

16.8%
Japan

6.2%
Korea (North & South)

5.0%
Indonesia

3.7%
Australia

57.1%
China

| | |
|---|---|
| Thailand | 2.6% |
| Malaysia | 2.0% |
| Phillippines | 1.8% |
| Vietnam | 1.7% |
| Singapore | 1.5% |
| Myanmar | 0.8% |
| Other | 0.8% |

US$30.0 trillion

SOURCE: IBISWORLD 01/09/15

China's dominance is now well recognised. Japan remains the second most important nation in the region, at 16.8% of the region's GDP, although this is being rapidly diluted due to Japan's negligible economic growth over the past quarter-century. Korea and Indonesia follow in third and fourth place, respectively, with similar GDP shares of around 5% to 6%.

Australia ranks fifth with just 3.7% of the region's GDP and that proportion is shrinking due to our subdued GDP growth of around 2.7% per annum, compared with the overall region's growth rate, which is almost double that. Australia's comparably weak growth is the result of a series of governments more concerned with infighting and/or politicking than leadership, vision and reform.

Population distribution carries nearly as much significance for Australia as does the region's economy. The second chart points to Australia's even lower position, with just 1.0% of the region's total population of 2.3 billion people. Our nearest neighbor, Indonesia, has a population 11 times greater than Australia's. China's population dominance — at around 62% — is even greater than its economic dominance.

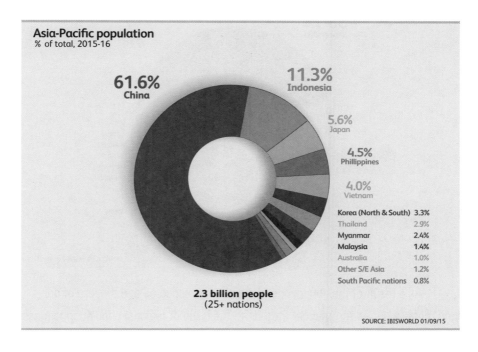

**Asia-Pacific population**
% of total, 2015-16

**61.6%**
China

**11.3%**
Indonesia

**5.6%**
Japan

**4.5%**
Phillippines

**4.0%**
Vietnam

| | |
|---|---|
| Korea (North & South) | 3.3% |
| Thailand | 2.9% |
| Myanmar | 2.4% |
| Malaysia | 1.4% |
| Australia | 1.0% |
| Other S/E Asia | 1.2% |
| South Pacific nations | 0.8% |

**2.3 billion people**
(25+ nations)

SOURCE: IBISWORLD 01/09/15

Australia's population — at 24 million — is so tiny that we could only stand one-deep with hands outstretched around our 36,000 kilometre coastline. By comparison, Indonesians could stand 11 deep and the Chinese population could stand almost 60 deep around our coastline!

Australia has a staggering one-third of the region's land mass and an equally staggering share of mineral resources. We are indeed richly endowed, even though the Organisation for Economic Co-operation and Development (OECD) rich nations group create more wealth through service industries than goods industries. Minerals, after all, have generated just under 10% of our GDP during the biggest mining boom in a hundred years, up from around 4% just 15 years ago.

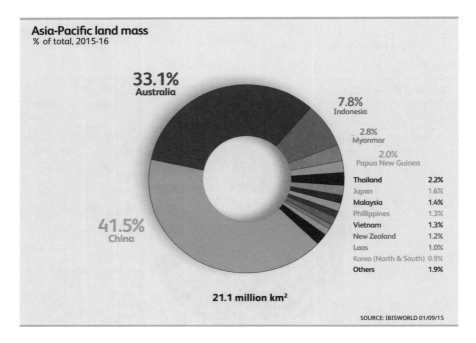

**Asia-Pacific land mass**
% of total, 2015-16

**33.1%**
Australia

**7.8%**
Indonesia

**2.8%**
Myanmar

**2.0%**
Papua New Guinea

| | |
|---|---|
| **Thailand** | **2.2%** |
| Japan | 1.6% |
| **Malaysia** | **1.4%** |
| Phillippines | 1.3% |
| **Vietnam** | **1.3%** |
| New Zealand | 1.2% |
| Laos | 1.0% |
| Korea (North & South) | 0.9% |
| **Others** | **1.9%** |

**41.5%**
China

**21.1 million km²**

SOURCE: IBISWORLD 01/09/15

As a result of the abundance of our natural resources and the size of our land mass, a dog-in-the-manger attitude to the issue of regional population fairness and balance will not earn Australia many friends and allies as this century unfolds.

Current forecasts are for an Australian population of more than 70 million by 2100 and perhaps a 'capacity limit' of somewhere between 140 and 200 million a century later. Still a tiny share of the Asia-Pacific region, let alone Asia at large (including the Indian subcontinent). Our population grew fivefold during the 20th century, but has slowed to a threefold growth rate so far in the 21st century.

In gratitude for our fortune, we need to display good neighbourliness. This includes open trade, high levels of international tourism (inbound and outbound) for cultural exchange and understanding, generous immigration levels (as we slowly move towards a Eurasian society this century and an Asian one by the 22nd century), the right diplomacy, and sound defence pacts and alliances. These are also elements of the defence of our nation and require vision, commitment, tolerance, patience and money.

Finally, in terms of perspective, we turn to the regional issue of food security. Below we have two charts: the disposition of arable land, and renewable water supplies in our region.

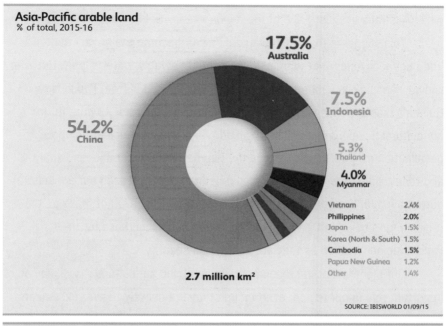

**Asia-Pacific arable land**
% of total, 2015-16

**17.5%**
**Australia**

**54.2%**
China

**7.5%**
Indonesia

**5.3%**
Thailand

**4.0%**
Myanmar

| | |
|---|---|
| Vietnam | 2.4% |
| Phillippines | 2.0% |
| Japan | 1.5% |
| Korea (North & South) | 1.5% |
| Cambodia | 1.5% |
| Papua New Guinea | 1.2% |
| Other | 1.4% |

**2.7 million km²**

SOURCE: IBISWORLD 01/09/15

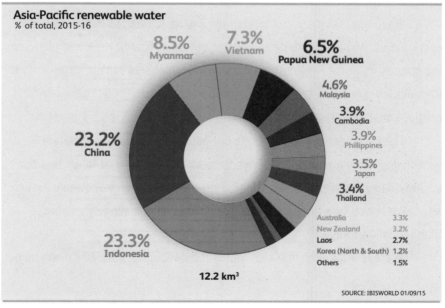

**Asia-Pacific renewable water**
% of total, 2015-16

**8.5%**
Myanmar

**7.3%**
Vietnam

**6.5%**
**Papua New Guinea**

**4.6%**
Malaysia

**3.9%**
Cambodia

**3.9%**
Phillippines

**3.5%**
Japan

**3.4%**
Thailand

**23.2%**
China

**23.3%**
Indonesia

| | |
|---|---|
| Australia | 3.3% |
| New Zealand | 3.2% |
| Laos | 2.7% |
| Korea (North & South) | 1.2% |
| Others | 1.5% |

**12.2 km³**

SOURCE: IBISWORLD 01/09/15

Again, we have a lot of arable land, nearly 18% of the region's total, with China dominating once more. However, arable land without enough water is a limiting factor. China has slightly less renewable water than Indonesia, while Australia has just 3.3% of the region's renewable water.

This suggests that Australia could never become the much-vaunted 'food bowl' of Asia — not with just 3% of the renewable water supply. But who knows, tapping the vast underground reserves flowing in from Papua New Guinea's massive renewable water into Australia's top end — where future agricultural development will be focused — and perhaps nuclear-powered desalination may yet help to bridge the gap between our arable land share and renewable water share. In the past century, we increased our agricultural output fivefold. We can do the same this century. This may not make us the region's food bowl, but it will be an important supply increase for the Asia-Pacific region, worried as they are about food security.

Our plentiful natural resources — mineral and agricultural — will play an important role in our region, even though they are unlikely to ever exceed an eighth of our GDP. But we will be perceived as 'rich' nevertheless.

There are many issues for Australia and its citizens to think about in the years ahead. And in a borderless world, it will be critical to think and plan from the outside-in, not the inside-out. While we were able to remain introverted for the past few centuries in a basically agrarian and uninformed region, we can't continue that way this century. The information revolution is seeing to that.

The inescapable issues include our population-carrying capacity — with respect to the region, not a myopic view of what is 'right for us and our ecology'. They equally include a sensible attitude to foreign investment, which after all is a two-way flow. Currently, we have been investing more abroad than the inflows anyway.

There is a third major issue: that is the need to identify which will be our competitive industries in an open and free-trading regional arena. We should not be scared or timid about that challenge. We only need to be competitive in one-quarter of our economy to pay for our imports, which will be between 20% and 25% of our GDP. These areas are not hard to find: tourism; service industries; and of course, our natural resources, some of the exports being in value-added (processed/manufactured) form. It promises to be a very prosperous century ahead.

But good and visionary government is essential for this journey.

# Generational Differences

*Company Director* magazine September 2015

Generational differences are very important to businesses these days, especially in terms of marketing and staffing. One size doesn't fit all, as they say. Consumers from each generation think and behave differently with their buying patterns and habits, and employees certainly view work in different ways if they are young compared with the 'older hands'.

There have been approximately 12 generations in Australia, of an average 20 years per cohort, since European settlement in 1788 and, surprisingly, six of those are still with us in 2015. Yes, half the generations that have existed over the last 227 years are still with us!

This is, of course, due to the much longer life expectancy today than in the early days of colonisation. The youngest generation alive today, those 13 years of age and younger, are expected to live until 100; whereas the generation of the 1890s had a life expectancy of just 38 years. This also explains why there was no divorce – there simply wasn't time.

## Introducing descriptors

Thomas Hobbes' description in 1651 of English lifetimes as 'solitary, poor, nasty, brutish, and short' was particularly true during wars. But it was probably also true for a lot of our citizens in the 1780s and for several decades later; and it is certainly accurate by today's life and living standards.

We only began to use descriptors for generations 50 years or so ago, and the US Government Census Bureau can inadvertently take the credit by referring to the post-WWII birth rate as a 'baby boom', hence the term 'baby boomers'. Prior to that you were the child, parent or grandparent generation.

Today's co-habiting generations in Australia, and their monikers and clipped descriptions, are shown in the chart below, together with their relative importance in numbers.

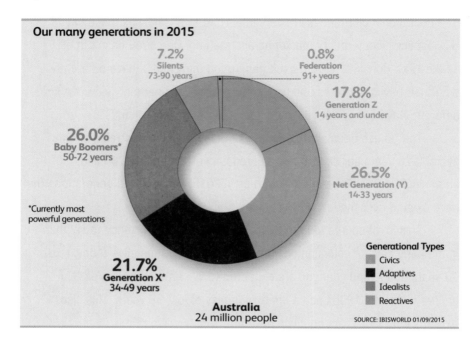

**Our many generations in 2015**

7.2%
Silents
73-90 years

0.8%
Federation
91+ years

17.8%
Generation Z
14 years and under

26.0%
Baby Boomers*
50-72 years

26.5%
Net Generation (Y)
14-33 years

*Currently most powerful generations

21.7%
Generation X*
34-49 years

**Australia**
24 million people

**Generational Types**
Civics
Adaptives
Idealists
Reactives

SOURCE: IBISWORLD 01/09/2015

Three of the generations are similar in size and importance: baby boomers, Generation X, and the Net Generation (variously called Gen Y or millennials). Most of them are in the workforce of 11.7 million, together with some veterans from the Silent Generation (people born from the mid-1920s to the early 1940s). All are consumers, topped up with the Federation Generation (older 'civics') and the younger generation Z. As a result, there are three to four generations of employees, and six generations of customers to address in our planning, tactics and operations.

## Generation breakdown

An anti-discrimination human resources regime means we could be employing three or four generations in our businesses; and that isn't easy to manage. But to try to please 24 million consumers spread across six generations is close to impossible, except for utilities and some commodities. We have to make choices and focus to succeed.

In the previous chart, the legend shows four descriptors matched to the colours on the pie chart. These descriptors are 'civics', 'adaptives', 'idealists' and 'reactives'. These descriptors were proposed by authors Strauss & Howe in their 1991 study entitled *Generations*.

Strauss and Howe had gone back hundreds of years in the US and found that there were four types of generations that followed each other in rotation over and over again.

In short, the conclusion was that civics are the wealth-creating and nation-building generation; the can-do generation, pragmatic and rationalist, but not endowed with a lot of social graces. The adaptives are generally silent and obedient, but a more socially aware generation; they adapt wealth-building to other social needs, and make good leaders. The idealists are the social visionary and idealistic generation who want to change the world now; they are humanists, social re-engineers and big spenders. The reactives are the conciliatory generation, consolidators of change and peacekeepers; they repair the economic damage of idealists and pave the way for the 'new civics'.

These characteristics are, of course, generalisations; and many other factors contribute to individual attitudinal and behavioural differences.

That said, the current Generation X, aged between 34 and 49, are proving better chief executive officers than the baby boomers, lifting average post-tax returns on shareholder funds from a prevailing 11% on average to 16%. By contrast, age, wisdom and courage are required of our successful political leaders, as measured by balanced budgets, full employment, strong economic growth and other nation-building factors.

## Benchmarking

Against these benchmarks, only one in four of our 76 national leaders since Captain Arthur Phillip have been all-round statesmen – albeit with imperfections and blind spots – and all were in the last fifth of their respective life expectancies.

Australia hasn't had one of these leaders for some years. There may be one in the wings. If not, we may have to wait for the aged industrious Gen Xers; but hopefully not that long.

Yes, there are generational differences. As directors, we have only a marginal impact on political leaders, but we ignore the differences in our customers and our workforce to the risk of the business. Managing these takes skill, tactics and tolerance.

# Is Another Recession Looming?

*Company Director* magazine August 2015

The word *recession* connotes fear, but the word *depression* suggests terror. A recession occurs when we have two or more quarters of negative economic growth, usually converting to a negative year overall; and a depression occurs when we have two or more negative years, usually four in a row for Australia.

Fortunately, we have had only four depressions in 227 years, the last one ending over 80 years ago in the 1930s; and fewer recessions than in the Industrial Age, when we had 20 over a 100-year period, or one every five years on average. However, we have only had two over the past 50 years since the new Infotronics Age began in 1965. The last one was 23 years ago, ending in 1992, as shown in the chart below. We return to the prospects of another one shortly.

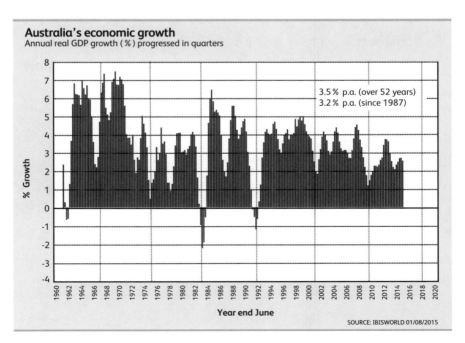

**Australia's economic growth**
Annual real GDP growth (%) progressed in quarters

3.5% p.a. (over 52 years)
3.2% p.a. (since 1987)

% Growth

Year end June

SOURCE: IBISWORLD 01/08/2015

## The facts

Half of today's workforce of 11.8 million has never experienced a recession in their working lifetime. This carries the risk of the boiling-frog syndrome, whereby complacency sets in, productivity growth slows, deficit spending can become a habit, workplace reforms are put off, and unemployment rises. This is Australia today, and Greece is an extreme example over a much longer period – two generations at least – and now a 'classic basket-case' as they say.

Strangely, we may be better off to have another recession sooner rather than later to correct the above drift, notwithstanding we have a very low national debt and a relatively modern economy. The nation has had reform paralysis for much too long; and that is dangerous, given our new economic and social homeland of Asia – the biggest, most dynamic and fastest growing region of the world – where we will be trading and competing for a century or more.

We need workplace reform involving penalty rates, contractualism (to reward on outputs, not inputs), more worker freedom and flexibility. We need reform in our parliament (Senate election protocols); in our federal budgeting (the deficit habit); in our taxes (GST in particular); in our negative productivity in government-owned activities (22% of the nation's GDP); in our society (more fairness, but also more self-reliance); in our energy policy area; and more.

## Cause of recession

However, while all these issues are important to our rising standard of living – and critical over the longer term – the cause of recessions lies elsewhere. Markets pull the economy (GDP) along, not production. There are three major sectors in the marketplace: overseas expenditure (our exports); consumption expenditure (households and government on our behalf); and capital expenditure.

Exports do turn negative in growth but rarely, and even those occasions have not been severe enough to trigger a recession in our new Infotronics Age over the past 50 years.

Consumption expenditure has not gone negative since WWII, so has never caused a recession in the lifetime of most Australians unless they are well over 75 years of age. One of the factors that has helped keep consumer spending in the positive zone is the dominance of services in household spending.

A century ago, goods once consumed more than two-thirds of household budgets, but now only occupy a fifth due to manufacturing productivity and, more recently, cheaper imports.

Indeed, in 2013, household spending on outsourced chores and services exceeded retail goods spending for the first time in history. Consumers are less likely to stop or curtail spending on services than goods, especially durables. They will still pay for electricity, insurance, health, education and even entertainment of one form or another. The facts show this to be true over the past six or more decades.

That leaves the only remaining market sector that can cause recessions: capital expenditure. The two recessions we have had in this new age were caused by a collapse of more than 8% in a given year. This happened in the 1982 to 1983 and 1991 to 1992 recessions.

## Business cycles

However, going back to the chart (page 113), dotted lines are shown around every eight-and-a-half years on average. This is what economists call the long business cycle; and it is at the end of each of these periods when our economy is susceptible or vulnerable to a collapse in capital expenditure.

In 2000, the Howard/Costello government averted a recession via the First Home Owner Grant initiative, which doubled in value the following year.

We missed a recession in 2008 to 2009 too, due to the massive backlog of mining capital expenditure. The Rudd Government's fiscal stimulus was unnecessary and a panic reaction. We didn't need any bolstering of consumer spending power: mortgage rates had collapsed from 9.25% to 5.25% from 2008, and petrol prices had fallen sharply. Together, these occurrences were enough to free up over $10,000 in after-tax money for the majority of households.

Perhaps the government should have encouraged the public to spend some of this money — rather than giving us more — and informed us that we were not going to experience a GFC as we had no national debt.

But the looming risk of a recession in 2017 to 2018 at the end of the current long business cycle is very real. Over 25% of our capital expenditure (itself 28% of GDP) was going to the mining boom until recently. At least 10% or more of this will have gone by 2018, so filling that hole is the challenge in avoiding a recession. Governments are largely aware of this risk, hence the drive into more infrastructure spending.

We have a couple of years to fill this hole, otherwise a probable recession is in train. But in the absence of serious reform vision, initiatives and courage, it may not be a bad thing if we had one to shake us out of lethargy. Another one 'we had to have', so to speak.

# Privatisation: What's all the Fuss About?

*IBISWorld Newsletter* April 2015

Privatisation has been a bête noire for many voters and the Labor Party in recent times, particularly at state elections, including the dramatic Queensland election earlier this year.

This seems odd given that over the past few decades, governments at federal, state and local levels have sold around $200 billion (in today's money terms) in assets – including the Commonwealth Bank, Qantas and more – without any lasting backlash.

In 2015, Australian governments at all three levels own and run businesses across 22% of the economy – a big share. It was a bigger share before the privatisation of banks, airlines, telcos, ports, some of the utilities, all of their manufacturing entities and many others, but these sales represented less than a tenth of their then-assets.

Indeed, in the early years of European settlement, with Australia being a convict colony, virtually the entire economy was made up of government-owned industries. So in Australia's case, we have come down to just over a fifth of gross domestic product (GDP) over the past 227 years rather than building up to that level.

The first chart overleaf shows those industry divisions in which our governments own businesses in 2015 – some where the government holds only a minority share of the industry or outsource operations, and some with 100% ownership of the industry.

The orange industry divisions total 41.7% of the economy, with governments controlling just over half that (22% of the economy as mentioned earlier), be they in the form of government business enterprises (GBEs) or

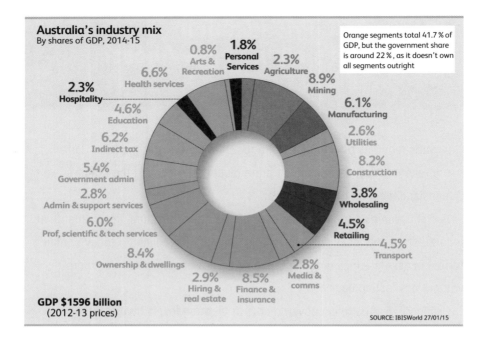

**Australia's industry mix**
By shares of GDP, 2014-15

Orange segments total 41.7% of GDP, but the government share is around 22%, as it doesn't own all segments outright

- 0.8% Arts & Recreation
- 1.8% Personal Services
- 2.3% Agriculture
- 8.9% Mining
- 6.6% Health services
- 2.3% Hospitality
- 4.6% Education
- 6.2% Indirect tax
- 5.4% Government admin
- 2.8% Admin & support services
- 6.0% Prof, scientific & tech services
- 8.4% Ownership & dwellings
- 2.9% Hiring & real estate
- 8.5% Finance & insurance
- 2.8% Media & comms
- 4.5% Transport
- 4.5% Retailing
- 3.8% Wholesaling
- 8.2% Construction
- 2.6% Utilities
- 6.1% Manufacturing

**GDP $1596 billion**
(2012-13 prices)

SOURCE: IBISWorld 27/01/15

general government activities (GGEs such as schools, museums etc.).

So, why did governments get into businesses, rather than just stick to governing the nation and its society and economy? There are several reasons:

- independence and security (public administration, defence, justice, police)
- national good (schools, health, public transport, other infrastructure, arts, parks etc)
- community sensitivity (postal services, savings banks)
- insufficient private capital access and/or low and slow returns (e.g. utilities, telecommunications)

The last two of these reasons are now not applicable. The community sensitivity issue has gone from such activities as postal services (now being outsourced or privatised) and banks (all now privatised and competitive). And capital markets are now very capable of raising any amount of capital (onshore and offshore) for private enterprise in any industry.

And yet, strangely, some Labor governments still support the notion that government assets are the 'people's assets', 'sacred cows' or icons, as witnessed in New South Wales for decades and in the Queensland state election this year. This is, of course, voodoo economics and jingoism, with collusion from the union movement. Utilities such as electricity, telecommunications and railways began life as GBEs because our capital markets were not mature enough to be able to provide the big and patient capital required by the private sector, as was possible in the United States.

It is not surprising that unions favour government ownership, as that is where most of their members are. The biggest union membership numbers are in health, education and the public service. But membership has fallen from around 55% of the workforce over 50 years ago to an expected 15% or less as we enter the third decade of this century, and will probably fall further to a single-digit level as we enter our fourth decade. So there is a strong and desperate rearguard action in play.

Governments are usually not very good at governing, let alone running businesses. IBISWorld analysis has suggested that at the federal level, only one in four leaders since 1788 have been outstanding statesmen, with the rest being ordinary, down to dysfunctional if not hopeless. State governments may have been marginally better. Ditto local government, the earthiest of the three levels. There has possibly been a similar balance in other democracies.

With power comes the opportunity for corruption, and this problem has been manifest in both local and state governments and unions up to the present day. To obviate this ever-present danger, a lot of government enterprises have become risk-averse, stolid and unproductive. Not a good mix.

Which leads to the questions of profitability and productivity.

Governments would have assets of over $2 trillion in Australia in 2015, earning pre-tax surpluses (of approximately $35 billion) yielding around 1.7%

on these assets: an extremely lazy return. Of course, the bulk of these assets are associated with not-for-profit (NFP) enterprises, but even many of the GBEs have poor returns by private sector standards. Does this have to be the case? Is it not possible to provide services at equal or lower costs and still make a reasonable return? Of course, as much – but not all – of the historic privatisation has demonstrated this to be possible. Should universities be sitting on $60 billion in assets, with revenue of less than half that investment ($28 billion) earning just several per cent return on net assets, with fees rising all the time?

That said, three of the 100 most profitable enterprises in Australia over the five years through 2012-13 were government entities, with an average return on net assets of a staggering 49%. But only three.

The picture in the productivity arena is not a pretty one either. The next chart shows the productivity growth by industry division over the five years through September 2014.

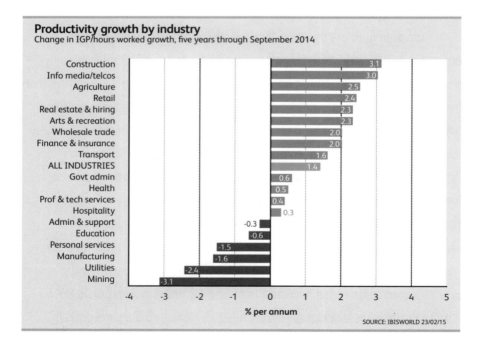

**Productivity growth by industry**
Change in IGP/hours worked growth, five years through September 2014

| Industry | % per annum |
|---|---|
| Construction | 3.1 |
| Info media/telcos | 3.0 |
| Agriculture | 2.5 |
| Retail | 2.4 |
| Real estate & hiring | 2.3 |
| Arts & recreation | 2.3 |
| Wholesale trade | 2.0 |
| Finance & insurance | 2.0 |
| Transport | 1.6 |
| ALL INDUSTRIES | 1.4 |
| Govt admin | 0.6 |
| Health | 0.5 |
| Prof & tech services | 0.4 |
| Hospitality | 0.3 |
| Admin & support | -0.3 |
| Education | -0.6 |
| Personal services | -1.5 |
| Manufacturing | -1.6 |
| Utilities | -2.4 |
| Mining | -3.1 |

SOURCE: IBISWORLD 23/02/15

Over this period, the nation's productivity growth averaged 1.4% per annum – that is, the output per hour of the nation's workforce increased by that amount each year, meaning that by the end of that period an hour of work yielded over 7% more than in 2009. The only worrying performances in the private sector were mining (now turned positive in 2014) and manufacturing (affected by the overvalued Australian dollar and blowtorch competition from China).

However, the NFP/government share of the economy went backwards at 0.4% per annum, suggesting that at the end of five years, the output per hour worked by government employees was generally 2% less than in 2009. Economists generally agree that measuring productivity in the services sectors of the economy, especially but not only government enterprises, is a bit wooly. But not so much that the above comparison doesn't stand up.

Then again, as with the profitability measure, there are some outstanding examples of government-owned enterprises with efficiency and courtesy, including road traffic authorities, Centrelink and many others.

Nevertheless, it is time to revisit the old chestnut of government ownership in terms of its justification. As mentioned earlier, we have witnessed a huge amount of privatisation over the past quarter-century, and an equally large amount of outsourcing (IT, delivery/distribution and even production). The nation needs more of this to further improve its productivity growth, particularly given enormous competitiveness in our home region, the Asia-Pacific, where over two-thirds (and increasing) of our trade takes place. And we need to work our assets much harder in terms of profitability, and improve the systems and productivity in the unionised workforce in these government activities.

We don't need jingoism and false gods, or nostalgia, to get in the way of necessary progress. Political and union rhetoric needs to be exposed for what it is.

# Progressing to a Peaceful World

*IBISWorld Newsletter* November 2014

The world is shrinking. Helping that process is fast internet communications, together with automated language interpretation. But there are still barriers to better understanding across the world's 7.3 billion people. And some of these barriers are scary, such as terrorism emanating from the Middle East. The main barriers to a more peaceful and wider trading society and economy are language, religion, politics, standard of living, climate and cultures (which are often a product of the other factors).

So, a numerical look at the dividing factors across the world's 230 nations and principalities can provide some perspective.

Language is a good start. The first chart shows the diversity of the spoken word, whether the result of the Tower of Babel, as claimed in the Book of Genesis, or springing from other origins.

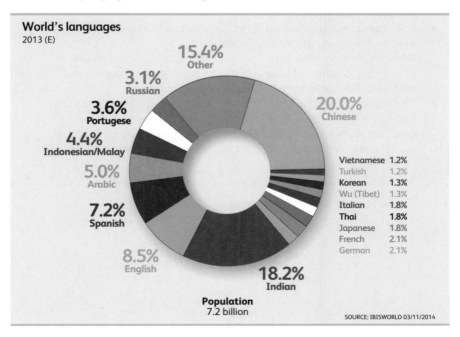

**World's languages**
2013 (E)

15.4% Other
3.1% Russian
3.6% Portugese
4.4% Indonesian/Malay
5.0% Arabic
7.2% Spanish
8.5% English
18.2% Indian
20.0% Chinese

| | |
|---|---|
| Vietnamese | 1.2% |
| Turkish | 1.2% |
| Korean | 1.3% |
| Wu (Tibet) | 1.3% |
| Italian | 1.8% |
| Thai | 1.8% |
| Japanese | 1.8% |
| French | 2.1% |
| German | 2.1% |

**Population**
7.2 billion

SOURCE: IBISWORLD 03/11/2014

Chinese and Indian languages are the big two as a first or second language, which is perhaps not surprising given that these are the world's two most populated nations. Yet English is the most commonly used, being either an official or spoken language across 188 countries, accounting for over 80% of all nations. Language can be a barrier to the integration of societies, but these days it is not as problematic as it once was due to the communications revolution.

Religion has been and remains more divisive, as demonstrated by the Crusades of the second millennium and other holy wars through the ages. The following exhibit elaborates on the hegemony exercised by many religions.

---

**Religious hegemony**

- Most religions have produced deviant, rebellious and fanatical branches over the millenniums, that have no recognition or respect for the founders' generally pacifist creeds, tenets or beliefs.
- The deviants have often gone to war in support or justification of their causes.
- The descriptors have included holy wars, sacred wars, crusades, conquests and jihads.
- The main religions involved in such deviant behavior have been or are Christianity, Islam and Judaism.
- Internecine wars have been the most devastating (e.g. Protestant vs Catholic, Sunnis vs Shiites), but wars between religions have also been horrific in terms of death and destruction.
- The leaders of such deviant branches are witch-doctors, narcissists and nihilists, and have been able to attract huge numbers of disaffected, cranky and low-intelligence (cannon-fodder) followers via their oratory, passion and promise of special afterlife happiness.

SOURCE: IBISWORLD 03/11/2014

---

The next chart shows the religious division extant in 2013.

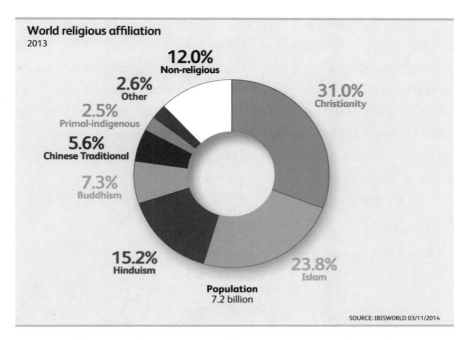

**World religious affiliation**
2013

- 12.0% Non-religious
- 2.6% Other
- 2.5% Primal-indigenous
- 5.6% Chinese Traditional
- 7.3% Buddhism
- 15.2% Hinduism
- 23.8% Islam
- 31.0% Christianity

**Population**
7.2 billion

SOURCE: IBISWORLD 03/11/2014

The founders of religions were, for the most part, well-intentioned and pacifists. It is a shame that some claimed inheritors have chosen to bastardise and fanaticise the original teachings. Terrorism, using religion as a justification, has been able to gain traction even in an advancing world economy and society, such as exists today – although this is perhaps not so surprising when divisions of wealth and the absence of true democracy still prevail in some parts of the world.

Many of the major religions' leaders and oligarchs have exercised hegemony over their followers and outsiders across millenniums. Those that have done so are basically witchdoctors and have often done far more harm than good, and in the name of God.

The witchdoctors, sadly, are alive and well in this new century, too.

As suggested earlier, political ideologies, oppression and poverty are all contributors to unrest, unhappiness, rebellion and fanaticism.

The below chart shows the world's political systems. At first sight, we could be cheered by the dominance of 'democracy', at over 70% of world population. However, this is misleading. A true and fair democracy is expensive. It requires a standard of living of over $25,000 per capita to ensure fair elections, an adequate and honest judiciary and reasonably corruption free military and police forces via taxation. It requires the tax capability to provide a measure of egalitarianism via support to the unemployed, aged, sick and illiterate members of society. Australia, as an advanced economy with a standard of living of $67,000 per capita, applies over $20,000 per capita (nearly one-third of our standard of living) via taxes to the above.

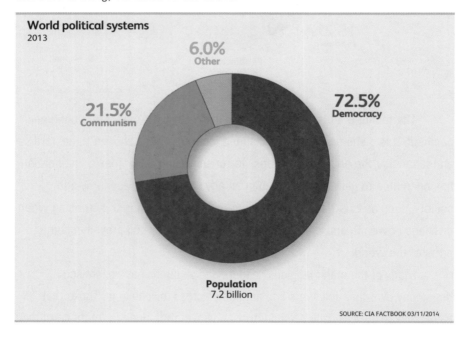

**World political systems**
2013

6.0%
Other

21.5%
Communism

72.5%
Democracy

**Population**
7.2 billion

SOURCE: CIA FACTBOOK 03/11/2014

So, we have a long way to go before democracy can actually work in poor and developing economies. Indeed, democracy achieved too early in a developing economy can arguably be worse than a benevolent 'guided democracy' or even a competent benevolent dictatorship.

Sadly, a number of so-called democracies around the world are headed by incompetent and greedy, if not malevolent, dictators.

While communism is on the wane, it still accounts for over one-fifth of world population, mainly in China, of course. With a standard of living of just $8,000 per capita, China is in no position to be able to yet provide the egalitarianism we now take for granted in the developed world. One day it will, but not for some decades. All it can do is provide – gradually – more benefits, more freedom and openness to its citizens.

In looking at standards of living (SOL), it is sobering to know the world average is around $12,000 per capita, compared with Australia's $67,000 per capita.

Further, the nations of the Organisation for Economic Co-operation and Development (OECD) (the so-called 'rich club') control 64% of the world's gross domestic product (GDP), with less than one-fifth of world population. Their average SOL is $36,000 per capita, ranging from Turkey and Mexico with $16,000 per capita to Luxembourg (with approximately $80,000 per capita).

This leaves over 80% of the world in the other 190-plus nations with an average SOL of just $5,900 per capita.

This is a serious division in the world, demanding much tolerance, knowledge transfer and generosity by the rich nations for all the right reasons. This is particularly necessary to avoid the damaging risks of envy, rebellion and terrorism to those nations that have already made it.

The world has had many wealth divisions over thousands of years. Sometimes these have arisen via the establishment of empires such as the Roman, Persian, Ottoman and British empires, and one could perhaps add the current American era (arguably a more benign power). Interestingly, the British Empire was built over a period of 150 years with annualised GDP growth of just 2%, followed by the rise of the United States over 100 years at 3.5% annualised GDP growth.

This makes China's current growth extraordinary, with over 8% annualised GDP growth during the past half-century, on its way to being the world's largest economy. Further, China has a population of about 1.4 billion, compared with Britain's 40 million people over two centuries ago and the United States' 70 million over a century ago, when they began their respective marches to supremacy.

Of further significance is the old East-West divide. This year, for the first time, the East has matched the economic power of the West, now 50/50 in terms of GDP in purchasing power parity (PPP) terms. The times they are a-changing, as is said.

A more encouraging development over the five decades since the end of the Industrial Age in the West (and most of the OECD) is the emergence of economic regions as depicted in the final chart.

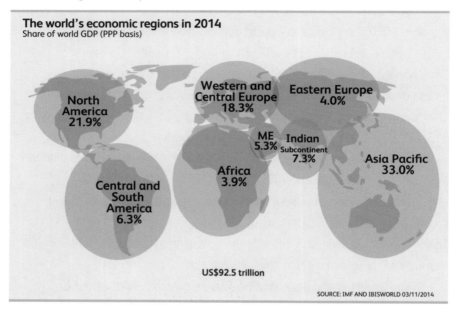

**The world's economic regions in 2014**
Share of world GDP (PPP basis)

North America 21.9%

Western and Central Europe 18.3%

Eastern Europe 4.0%

ME 5.3%

Indian Subcontinent 7.3%

Asia Pacific 33.0%

Africa 3.9%

Central and South America 6.3%

US$92.5 trillion

SOURCE: IMF AND IBISWORLD 03/11/2014

During this new era, extending from the mid-1960s to the middle of the 21st century, the world's 230 nations are gradually coalescing into eight regions. This is bringing more peace, prosperity, good-neighbourliness, trade and social interchange via travel than the world has ever seen. The Middle East may take longer than other regions due to the intense racial and long-standing religious animosity. And Africa is taking a long time to emerge from poverty, disease and corrupt leadership.

So, not yet a world without divisions and differences, but progress all the same.

# What is the World Coming To?

*IBISWorld Newsletter* August 2014

In case some think the world is going to pot, it is well to remember that just 50 years ago in 1964:

- We didn't live as long (67 years vs. 78 years for men and 84 for women)
- We were hung-up and embarrassed by anything to do with sex
- Domestic violence, rape and paedophilia went unreported
- Septic tanks were still common, if not the norm
- No freeways, domestic jet planes, mobile phones or internet
- Only black and white TV, which cost over $2,800 in today's money!
- The drink scene was awful (six o'clock pub swill, paralytic drunks)
- Shops closed Saturday afternoons, Sundays and public holidays
- There was slow-food but no fast-food outlets
- There was no universal superannuation scheme
- Few went to university (50,000 vs. 1.4 million today)
- There were no cures for cancer and lots of other health problems
- Who could you outsource household chores to?

A glance at the first chart overleaf reminds us how much better off we have become in economic and financial terms.

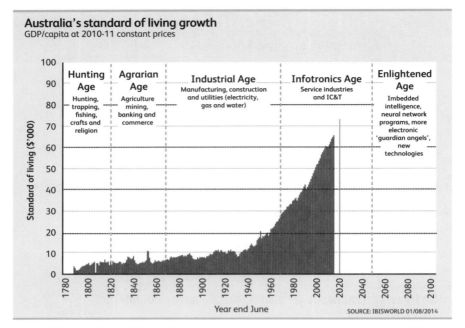

## Australia's standard of living growth
GDP/capita at 2010-11 constant prices

**Hunting Age** — Hunting, trapping, fishing, crafts and religion

**Agrarian Age** — Agriculture mining, banking and commerce

**Industrial Age** — Manufacturing, construction and utilities (electricity, gas and water)

**Infotronics Age** — Service industries and IC&T

**Enlightened Age** — Imbedded intelligence, neural network programs, more electronic 'guardian angels', new technologies

Year end June

SOURCE: IBISWORLD 01/08/2014

Our standard of living is nearly three times greater than it was in 1964, when the old Industrial Age was giving way to our new age.

The following two lists serve as further reminders of differences between yesteryear and nowadays.

### Yesterday's lifestyles
In the Industrial Age from 1865 to the mid-1960s

- **Dad was at work, mum was at home** (with 3 to 6 kids)
- **One-car households** (many none)
- **Long careers for men, and the gold watch**
- **Strict rules about sex, blaspheming and other stuff**
- **High street shopping** (grocer, butcher, etc.), **no centres**
- **Do-it-yourself everything, in and around the home**
- **The corner pub** (weekdays), **sport** (Saturday arvo)
- **Church and the midday roast** (Sundays)
- **Cinema, radio, a piano** (maybe) **and cards as entertainment**
- **Holidays** (Christmas) **by staying with relatives or friends**
- **Electricity, the telephone, washing machines, household gadgets, mum's sewing room, dad's shed and the BBQ**
- **And crossword puzzles arrived in 1914, now >100 years old!**

SOURCE: IBISWORLD 01/08/2014

**Today's lifestyles**
In the New Age from 1965 to the 2050s

- **Home ownership still dominant (66%), but leasing on the rise**
- **Dad and mum at work, with 1-3 kids** (thank God for mobiles)
- **Outsourcing of household services and chores**
- **New tribalism** (no longer based as much on neighbourhood)
- **More marriages due to longer lives** (but average still 20 years)
- **Less divorces than four decades ago** (yes, really)
- **The internet** (social media, email, information, banking, shopping)
- **Mobile telephones, tablets, other electronic gadgets**
- **Digital/3D colour TV** (including pay TV), **radio** (FM, DAB, internet)
- **Electronic guardian angels** (pacemakers, Cochlear, ABS brakes)
- **Sport all the time** (including on TV) **and new gambling options**
- **Modern clubs, pubs, hotels, casinos and entertainment**
- **Frequent holidays** (esp. short breaks) **and lots of overseas travel**

SOURCE: IBISWORLD 01/08/2014

With age comes the temptation to reminisce about the so-called 'good old days'. Some 20% of the population is now over 65 years – although this is not necessarily 'old' or 'aged' – and this is heading for 28% by the middle of this century. This age group made up only 7% of the population in 1914, 100 years ago.

So when we hear the lament about 'what is the world coming to', it is often a case of misplaced nostalgia, a failure to recognise progress and confusing habits with values.

The trouble with habits is:

- Different generations have or develop different habits, customs and traditions (all of which are habits anyway), but these are not to be confused with values such as love, respect and concern for others, which are timeless
- People confuse habits and values all the time, leading to squabbles and arguments for no useful purpose
- So, when we hear people defending a tradition, we should be suspicious, as it is often a long habit that has passed its use-by date and is without any real value!

Habits, customs and traditions – all being habits with different longevities – have use-by dates, and examples of habits that are not values include:

- Home ownership (more are leasing and owning doesn't 'save marriages')
- Doing housework (more of it is now being outsourced)
- Renovations, maintenance and gardening (ditto)
- One long career (we will have many)
- Same place for holidays (more variety is now the norm)
- Studying mostly on campus for tertiary education (the online revolution?)
- Criminalising drugs (should be legalising them to reduce deaths and crime)

Living longer means living with and respecting a wide variety of habits and traditions across different generations. After all, habits and traditions are comfortable to each generation. The really important thing is to distinguish them from the values that are truly worth promoting and defending at all costs.

We have six generations alive today, as the next chart reminds us.

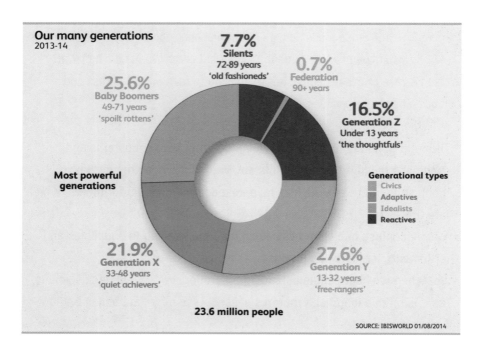

**Our many generations**
2013-14

**7.7%**
Silents
72-89 years
'old fashioneds'

**0.7%**
Federation
90+ years

**25.6%**
Baby Boomers
49-71 years
'spoilt rottens'

**16.5%**
Generation Z
Under 13 years
'the thoughtfuls'

**Most powerful generations**

**Generational types**
■ Civics
■ Adaptives
■ Idealists
■ Reactives

**21.9%**
Generation X
33-48 years
'quiet achievers'

**27.6%**
Generation Y
13-32 years
'free-rangers'

**23.6 million people**

SOURCE: IBISWORLD 01/08/2014

We have never had so many generations alive at the same time, so this number magnifies the dilemma of differing habits, customs and traditions. We see this challenge reflected in politics with more segmentation of minor parties, in businesses needing to almost micro-manage the different workforce generations and certainly in consumer markets.

But we need to be very careful in defining 'old' or 'aged' these days. What is old? At 65 years of age:

- **In 1800, you were dead 27 years ago**
- **In 1900, you were dead 12 years ago**
- **In 2000, you had between 12 and 15 years to go**
- **In 2014, 65 is the new 45 of the 1930s**
- **In 2100, you may be only two-thirds through your life!**

Even at 70 years of age, especially towards the middle of this century, most people will still be working, probably part-time, and will be fit and healthy. After all, only a very small proportion of the workforce is in physically demanding work nowadays, and even then there are OH&S safeguards for the health and longevity of such workers. Most jobs are cerebral, and the only way to wear out the brain is to stop using it!

One in four children born in 2001 are expected to live to a hundred – longer for women. Life expectancy is increasing by two to three years per decade, so we need to keep raising the age definition of 'old'.

What is extraordinary is that today's generation of workers – and future generations of workers for that matter – will still work the same number of hours per lifetime as did all generations over the past several centuries: approximately 130,000 hours. Today, males average 80,000 paid hours of work and 50,000 unpaid hours (i.e. home activities, volunteering and charity). The total is the same for females, but the ratios are different.

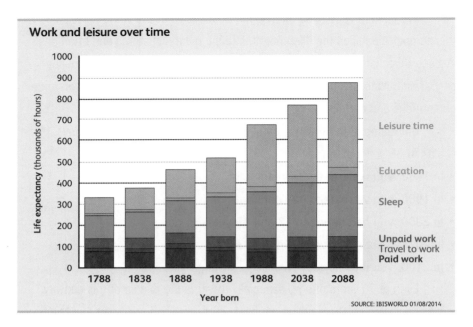

**Work and leisure over time**

Life expectancy (thousands of hours) vs Year born

Categories (bottom to top): Paid work, Travel to work, Unpaid work, Sleep, Education, Leisure time

SOURCE: IBISWORLD 01/08/2014

What has changed is that we spread the paid work over 50 years at half the number of hours per year compared with the early 19th century, when it was 25 years at twice the annual number of hours worked. Ditto the unpaid hours, which are now spread over nearly 70 years instead of around 30 years, but with the same total (50,000 hours on average).

But now we have over 310,000 hours of leisure or discretionary time in our lifetimes, compared with just 75,000 hours back in the early 1900s – that's more than four times the leisure. Indeed, our total leisure time nowadays is as long as the entire lifetime of an early English settler, and it is 42% of our life compared with half that proportion for our forebears.

So, the good old days? We are living in them!

# Australia in Global Perspective

*IBISWorld Newsletter* May 2014

Australia is a unique nation, as perhaps many of the world's 230 nations and protectorates could claim. Along with New Zealand, we are an English-speaking, largely Caucasian society in a world region that is ethnically very different. Yet a few centuries ago, both nations were different anyway: New Zealand with a society of Polynesian origins and Australia with an isolated Aboriginal ethnicity dating back over five millenniums. Both nations have progressed after colonisation by the British to be among the wealthiest in per capita terms in the Asia-Pacific region.

The first economic perspective is shown in the chart below. Australia is currently the 12th largest economy in the world, with 2.1% of its gross domestic product (GDP). Yet with a population of just over 23 million, it is the 57th most populous. New Zealand is 64th in economic size and 125th in population. Our landmasses rank 6th (very close to China, which is 4th) and 76th respectively.

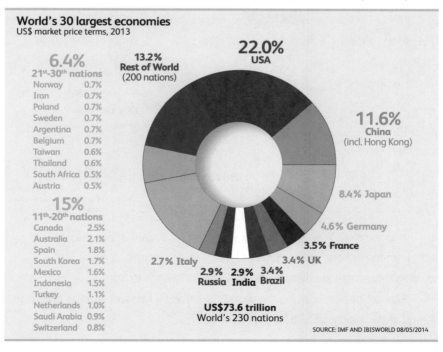

**World's 30 largest economies**
US$ market price terms, 2013

**6.4%**
21st-30th nations
| | |
|---|---|
| Norway | 0.7% |
| Iran | 0.7% |
| Poland | 0.7% |
| Sweden | 0.7% |
| Argentina | 0.7% |
| Belgium | 0.7% |
| Taiwan | 0.6% |
| Thailand | 0.6% |
| South Africa | 0.5% |
| Austria | 0.5% |

**15%**
11th-20th nations
| | |
|---|---|
| Canada | 2.5% |
| Australia | 2.1% |
| Spain | 1.8% |
| South Korea | 1.7% |
| Mexico | 1.6% |
| Indonesia | 1.5% |
| Turkey | 1.1% |
| Netherlands | 1.0% |
| Saudi Arabia | 0.9% |
| Switzerland | 0.8% |

**13.2%**
**Rest of World**
(200 nations)

**22.0%**
USA

**11.6%**
China
(incl. Hong Kong)

8.4% Japan

4.6% Germany

3.5% France

3.4% UK

2.7% Italy

2.9% Russia   2.9% India   3.4% Brazil

**US$73.6 trillion**
World's 230 nations

SOURCE: IMF AND IBISWORLD 08/05/2014

Our economic importance in the previous chart is measured in what is called US$ market price terms. But the picture changes when we use purchasing power parity (PPP) terms. The second of these measures is the result of pricing all goods and services according to volumes, with the price of such products being as they would be in the United States, regardless of where they are produced.

The chart below shows the different pecking order when this more accepted measure is used. Australia eases back to 17th on this basis. Other differences include China's closeness to the United States, India being now bigger than Japan, Russia moving from 9th to 6th, and Mexico displacing Italy in the Top 10.

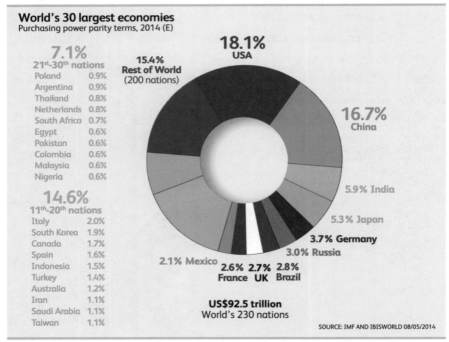

**World's 30 largest economies**
Purchasing power parity terms, 2014 (E)

**7.1%**
21st-30th nations

| | |
|---|---|
| Poland | 0.9% |
| Argentina | 0.9% |
| Thailand | 0.8% |
| Netherlands | 0.8% |
| South Africa | 0.7% |
| Egypt | 0.6% |
| Pakistan | 0.6% |
| Colombia | 0.6% |
| Malaysia | 0.6% |
| Nigeria | 0.6% |

**14.6%**
11th-20th nations

| | |
|---|---|
| Italy | 2.0% |
| South Korea | 1.9% |
| Canada | 1.7% |
| Spain | 1.6% |
| Indonesia | 1.5% |
| Turkey | 1.4% |
| Australia | 1.2% |
| Iran | 1.1% |
| Saudi Arabia | 1.1% |
| Taiwan | 1.1% |

15.4%
**Rest of World**
(200 nations)

**18.1%**
USA

**16.7%**
China

5.9% India

5.3% Japan

**3.7% Germany**

3.0% Russia

2.1% Mexico

**2.6% 2.7% 2.8%**
**France UK Brazil**

**US$92.5 trillion**
World's 230 nations

SOURCE: IMF AND IBISWORLD 08/05/2014

Impressively, Australia has the 4th highest standard of living (GDP per capita) among nations with a population of 1 million people or more. But including those with smaller populations, we ease back to 8th.

Our net national debt is the world's 3rd lowest, having been the lowest at the end of the Howard/Costello regime in 2007.

# Standard of living ladder
GDP per capita, 2013

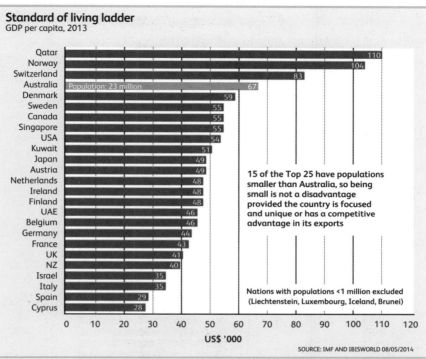

15 of the Top 25 have populations smaller than Australia, so being small is not a disadvantage provided the country is focused and unique or has a competitive advantage in its exports

Nations with populations <1 million excluded (Liechtenstein, Luxembourg, Iceland, Brunei)

Population: 23 million

US$ '000

SOURCE: IMF AND IBISWORLD 08/05/2014

# Government net debt
20 largest nations, 2013

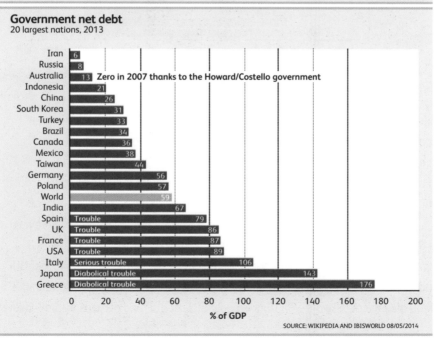

Zero in 2007 thanks to the Howard/Costello government

% of GDP

SOURCE: WIKIPEDIA AND IBISWORLD 08/05/2014

The dysfunctional and largely incompetent Rudd/Gillard/Rudd governments dropped the nation to third and left a legacy of budget deficit spending that dropped Australia again from the best in the world to 11th. There is no serious threat in the current levels; it's just a pity about the direction, which needs reversing. Fortunately, we are still up with the top nations in both regards.

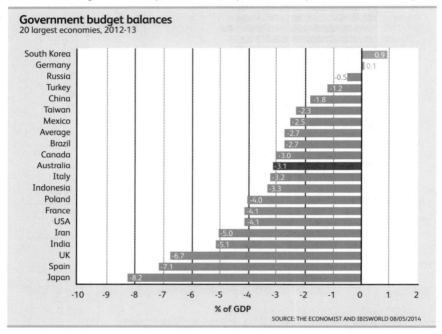

**Government budget balances**
20 largest economies, 2012-13

| Country | % of GDP |
|---|---|
| South Korea | 0.9 |
| Germany | 0.1 |
| Russia | -0.5 |
| Turkey | -1.2 |
| China | -1.8 |
| Taiwan | -2.3 |
| Mexico | -2.5 |
| Average | -2.7 |
| Brazil | -2.7 |
| Canada | -3.0 |
| Australia | -3.1 |
| Italy | -3.2 |
| Indonesia | -3.3 |
| Poland | -4.0 |
| France | -4.1 |
| USA | -4.1 |
| Iran | -5.0 |
| India | -5.1 |
| UK | -6.7 |
| Spain | -7.1 |
| Japan | -8.2 |

SOURCE: THE ECONOMIST AND IBISWORLD 08/05/2014

Our nation's unemployment has slipped from full employment (less than 5% unemployed) to just under 6%, which puts us 8th among the largest economies in the world. But we were comfortably above these economies' average of 7.2% at the end of 2013, let alone the entire world's average of around 12% or Spain and Greece's diabolical levels of more than 25% unemployment with youth unemployment at twice that!

As mentioned in previous newsletters, we are the second lowest taxed nation in the Organisation for Economic Co-operation and Development (OECD), far and away from the debilitating tax levels of the European Union (mostly over 40% of GDP) and nations such as Brazil and Japan (whose taxes are nevertheless close to the OECD average of 37% of GDP). Ours is under 30% of GDP, and perhaps a little too low.

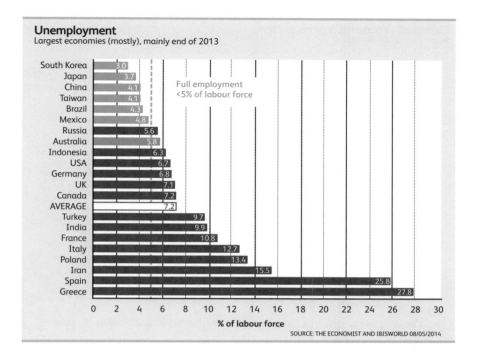

**Unemployment**
Largest economies (mostly), mainly end of 2013

| Country | % of labour force |
|---|---|
| South Korea | 3.0 |
| Japan | 3.7 |
| China | 4.1 |
| Taiwan | 4.1 |
| Brazil | 4.3 |
| Mexico | 4.8 |
| Russia | 5.6 |
| Australia | 5.8 |
| Indonesia | 6.3 |
| USA | 6.7 |
| Germany | 6.8 |
| UK | 7.1 |
| Canada | 7.2 |
| AVERAGE | 7.2 |
| Turkey | 9.7 |
| India | 9.9 |
| France | 10.8 |
| Italy | 12.7 |
| Poland | 13.4 |
| Iran | 15.5 |
| Spain | 25.8 |
| Greece | 27.8 |

Full employment <5% of labour force

**% of labour force**

SOURCE: THE ECONOMIST AND IBISWORLD 08/05/2014

Our interest rates are middle-of-the-road, with 10-year bond rates at 4%.

Perhaps the most unflattering ranking for Australia going into 2014 is in global competitiveness. The World Economic Forum placed us 21st. That said the gaps are not large among the top 25 nations, with Switzerland top of the ladder at 5.7 versus our 5.1 at 21st and South Korea at 25th with a score of 5.0. Nevertheless, we have been sliding down the ladder in the absence of any meaningful economic, business and labour reform for most of the past 7 to 8 years. Early signs are that this challenge is understood at the federal level and by some state governments.

Apart from the intrinsic necessity to constantly adjust, reform and progress in terms of productivity and new industries, our presence in the Asia-Pacific region is an added incentive. As the final chart shows, our region is the biggest of the eight that make up this year's GDP of over US$92.5 trillion. It is also the fastest growing (twice the world's average) and the most competitive.

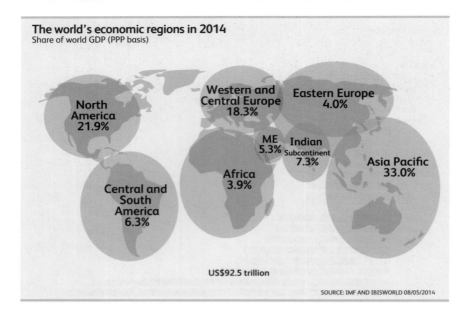

**The world's economic regions in 2014**
Share of world GDP (PPP basis)

North America 21.9%

Western and Central Europe 18.3%

Eastern Europe 4.0%

ME 5.3%

Indian Subcontinent 7.3%

Asia Pacific 33.0%

Africa 3.9%

Central and South America 6.3%

US$92.5 trillion

SOURCE: IMF AND IBISWORLD 08/05/2014

We only need look at China's neighbour, Japan, and its failure to reform after the financial collapse of 1989 and the subsequent economic recession to see how the mighty can fall.

Australia is much smaller than Japan of course (except in landmass). Our population is just 1% of the region and our economy is some 4%. But our potential is enormous.

We owe it to ourselves and future generations to be much more forward looking, reformist and productive than we have been lately. It is previous generations that have gotten Australia to its high ranking across so many measures today. But living off those crown jewels is not the right way forward.

Almost certainly, Australia will be a Eurasian society by the end of this century, with a population of about 72 million by 2100 if growth stays at a modest 1.3% per annum (much less than in the 20th century). The other challenge will be becoming a Eurasian economy, rather than a European one given the mess that the West is in. It is sobering to know the Asia-Pacific region will be bigger in economic output than all the Western nations combined within a decade. Add in the Indian subcontinent – which is then the Asia mega-region – and it is a lay-down misère, as they say in card games.

# The Closure of Car Making

*IBISWorld Newsletter* March 2014

The closure of car making within three years has led to a debate about protectionism and subsidies: a necessary debate in a country like ours that hasn't seen any meaningful economic or labour reforms for nearly a decade. Fruit processing and other industries are in this arena too.

The jingoism, hyperbole, deception, self-interest and just plain muddled thinking that have emerged over the past month or so are a shame, when clear-thinking and forward-looking ideas and policies are so important.

The planned car manufacturing industry closure by 2017, which began with Ford under the Labor Government and now includes GM Holden and Toyota under the Coalition Government, is long overdue. These three companies have been running losses on the manufacturing side of their businesses (but not their importing of cars) for many years. This is despite receiving billions of dollars in subsidies.

So who wins? The car manufacturers didn't, losing money every year and at least half their shareholder funds over the past five years. The taxpayers didn't, as the money could have gone into growing industries, not one that has been shedding jobs for years, and cars would have been cheaper for them (as imports). Workers aren't winning by staying in a dying industry, risking their future livelihood by becoming too old to reskill and move into a viable industry.

And to keep an industry that is making cars that few people want to buy is not smart. It is idiocy.

The first chart overleaf puts the lie to there being no jobs for such 'poor dislocated workers' — the nation is creating around five times more jobs than it is losing!

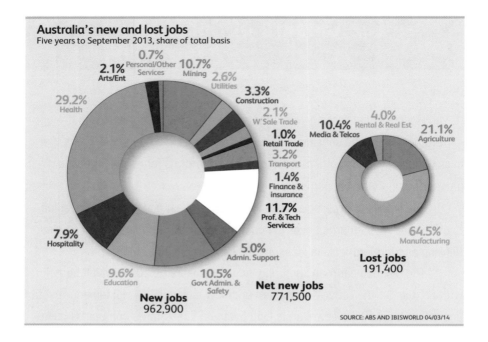

**Australia's new and lost jobs**
Five years to September 2013, share of total basis

- 0.7% Personal/Other Services
- 2.1% Arts/Ent
- 10.7% Mining
- 2.6% Utilities
- 3.3% Construction
- 29.2% Health
- 2.1% W'Sale Trade
- 1.0% Retail Trade
- 3.2% Transport
- 1.4% Finance & insurance
- 11.7% Prof. & Tech Services
- 7.9% Hospitality
- 5.0% Admin. Support
- 9.6% Education
- 10.5% Govt Admin. & Safety

**New jobs** 962,900
**Net new jobs** 771,500

- 10.4% Media & Telcos
- 4.0% Rental & Real Est
- 21.1% Agriculture
- 64.5% Manufacturing

**Lost jobs** 191,400

SOURCE: ABS AND IBISWORLD 04/03/14

The number of jobs that will be lost in three years' time is really tiny: less than 50,000 (but mistakenly said to be as high as 100,000). The nation creates that many new jobs every three months! There are three years to think about or get a new job, before the closure of car makers' and part makers' plants, which suggests that the pain and disruption are greatly exaggerated. Adelaide has already well and truly recovered from Mitsubishi's closure years ago.

To suggest the nation must have a car industry because of its skill base is, of course, bunkum. It is to mourn the loss of the horse-drawn ploughs of nearly a century ago (displaced by tractors), or the horse-drawn carts of 60 to 70 years ago (replaced by cars), or mechanical watches (now replaced by electronic ones) or outside dunnies (replaced by inside sewered toilets). Panel-beating repairs – an after-market activity – have of course been modernised with panel replacement.

We can wildly overstate the necessity of preserving 'skills'.

Cars are likely to be displaced by electric vehicles within decades anyway, some of which, ironically, may be produced here.

We are human beings, so we will always have emotions, loyalties and foibles. We tend to forget, as we should, that our car manufacturers are all foreign-owned and we are inclined to see them as Australian-owned icons, encouraged by the manufacturers themselves. Ownership, however, is irrelevant. If an industry is not viable, it doesn't matter who owns it.

And to blame a government of the day for the collapse of an industry, be it car making, fruit canning, clothing manufacturing, making horse-drawn ploughs or the hundreds of other activities that are now (or soon to be) history, is gormless or gutless politics and sometimes dumb media opinion. Even the car makers themselves are rightly attributing the problems to lack of economies of scale, exchange rates and labour costs (i.e. trying to compete with emerging economies), rather than blaming a government.

So protectionism can be a pernicious element in an economy and society. But there are good and bad sides to protectionism.

People and businesses need help and protection from time to time, if not all the time in some cases. Some $25 billion is spent on defence, $10 billion on police and over a quarter of a billion on emergency services each year. So just under $36 billion, or 2.6% of our gross domestic product (GDP), is spent to protect lives and property from external threats, crime and natural disasters. Money mostly well spent.

Then there is another sort of protectionism: welfare for the disadvantaged, which we also provide via our taxes. In 2013-14, we will provide almost $140 billion in support to the aged, unemployed, disabled and disadvantaged. And because we are an advanced and civilised society, we will also provide over $105 billion in health support and over $45 billion in education support.

So safety, welfare, health and literacy come with a bill of $337 billion, or about one-quarter of the nation's annual wealth creation (GDP). This is 87% of the nation's government income from taxes and running businesses (utilities, transport, etc.).

Australia's taxes – at 28% of GDP – make it the second-lowest taxing

nation of all advanced economies in the Organisation for Economic
Co-operation and Development (OECD).

Some are closer to 50% – such as Denmark and France – with another
five countries over 40%. The average is 37% for the advanced nations, so we
are a lowly taxed nation and a long way away from being a nanny state.

We are not over-protected at this juncture.

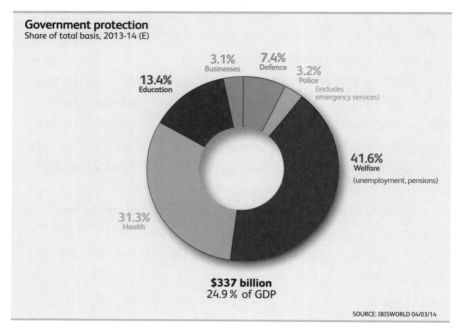

**Government protection**
Share of total basis, 2013-14 (E)

3.1% Businesses

7.4% Defence

3.2% Police (includes emergency services)

13.4% Education

41.6% Welfare (unemployment, pensions)

31.3% Health

**$337 billion**
24.9% of GDP

SOURCE: IBISWORLD 04/03/14

Once upon a time, the business protection element, currently 3% of all
protection shown on the second chart, was in place to help industries – and
therefore the economy and employment – to grow. This was particularly the
case early in the 20th century, especially for manufacturing and especially via
tariff protection and embargoes. These days, much, if not most, is for lost
causes.

Compared with the total spending on protection, the amount of money
isn't all that much: just under $11 billion in 2013-14 and 0.8% of GDP. But
that would be better used to help the growth of tomorrow's industries, not

yesterday's. And we are lagging our normal economic growth of 3.5% by that 0.8% of GDP amount anyway in the 21$^{st}$ century.

There are two negatives arriving out of protecting yesterday's industries. The first is that it provides fiscal morphine to uncompetitive, if not dying, industries and their businesses, rather than a stimulus to growing industries. It can encourage many industries and their businesses to hold out their hand.

The nation either wants to go forward, embracing the new and being prepared to abandon the old, or will let nostalgia, rent-seeking and jingoism take us backward to the so-called 'good old days', which weren't, except by comparing them to even older times. This sort of justification, taken to absurdity, would lead us back to the Neanderthal Age.

We hear that a nation cannot survive without a manufacturing sector. A glance at the next chart puts the lie to this populist claim – our nation has seen an exponential climb in our standard of living with the declining importance of both agriculture and manufacturing.

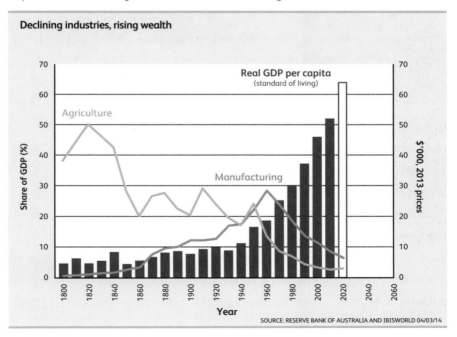

**Declining industries, rising wealth**

SOURCE: RESERVE BANK OF AUSTRALIA AND IBISWORLD 04/03/14

Agriculture was once 50% of our GDP, even 25% in 1950, and is now 2%. Manufacturing was once 29% of GDP (in 1960) and is now just over 7%.

Interestingly, both these old-and-bold industries are expected to experience a renaissance of sorts during the 21st century – not back to their once-dominant positions in the economy, but a revival nevertheless, in a new form.

Agriculture will emerge more like mining, by going corporate, capital-intensive, Asian export oriented and largely foreign owned, as the mining industry did 50 years ago.

Agriculture cannot survive and become even a small food-bowl in its present Small to Medium Enterprises (SME) ownership form, as heartless as that might sound; it has to follow the lessons of mining. The blocking of the Graincorp sale to ADM was regressive in this regard, showing ignorance of where our future lies. But Banjo Paterson, Dorothea Mackellar, Henry Lawson and other icons will survive this coming revolution, at least in continuing folklore and legend.

The manufacturing sector will become a very different sector too, but in many cases made up of more medium-size enterprises with high-tech/3D technology where applicable and more IT-based than the old craft and engineering skills that many think must be retained at all costs (but not so).

Franchising systems and international strategic alliances will be critical elements in the renaissance of both these industries.

A nation must be prepared to shed the old in favour of the new. We see that challenge in retailing in the first decades of the new century. That industry has gone through three revolutions over several centuries: the move to specialty stores in the 1820s, the move to chain stores in the 1890s and the move to self-service in the 1960s. We can hear the bleating today of the winners of that last revolution as the fourth revolution is descending like a tsunami in the form of online retailing. It is vital that the marketplace and progressive technology win, not the regressive players demanding protection.

Ironically, some of the nation's most profitable medium to large companies are in our declining and toughest industries. Of the 100 most profitable companies in terms of ROSF (returns on shareholder funds, after tax), averaged over the five years through 2012-13, a surprising 21 were in manufacturing (weighted average ROSF of 53.1%), seven in retailing (42.1%) and one in agriculture (34.7%). These returns compare with some 14.0% for all the medium to large enterprises. As is said, there is no such thing as bad industries, only bad companies. So why protect the bad ones?

The second negative with protecting declining industries is the fortunes of the workers, as raised earlier. By protecting industries beyond their use-by date, there is a huge risk that the same thing happens to workers, who may have 10 to 15 years of working life ahead of them. There is a double jeopardy if such workers are in country or coastal areas, far from major centres, that mitigate against daily commuting to other sorts of work.

The textile, clothing and footwear industry was a case of excessive protectionism for too long, and staffed by a lot of migrant women who found it near-impossible to reskill for another season in their working life.

History tells us that it is prudent for people to take charge of their own destiny more than they tend to do these days. To blindly believe a government of the day, an employer or a union is dangerous, even when they are sincere in their promises of a safe future. It is to tempt fate.

Forward planning, reskilling and even moving one's house are all necessities in the world of today where there are likely to be five or six careers or seasons in a working life of 50 to 55 years.

Clearly there will always be enough new jobs over time to replace those lost, as pointed out earlier. So to suggest wages should be lowered to save an industry is voodoo economics; no country got rich by keeping jobs that should go to poorer yet emerging economies. Competing with them is to go backwards. And lose anyway. At the same time, productivity growth can maintain wages for a shrinking number of workers for some years in some industries.

But protectionism with taxpayer money for yesterday's industries is a lost cause, and ultimately does more harm than good.

The future is too prospective and too exciting to let nostalgia or vested interests spoil the party.

# Getting Richer

*IBISWorld Newsletter* February 2013

The average household in Australia is earning more and getting wealthier by the year and decade, but the growing wealth is less to do with housing assets than financial assets, despite the global financial crisis. The first chart shows the climbing incomes in both nominal and constant price terms.

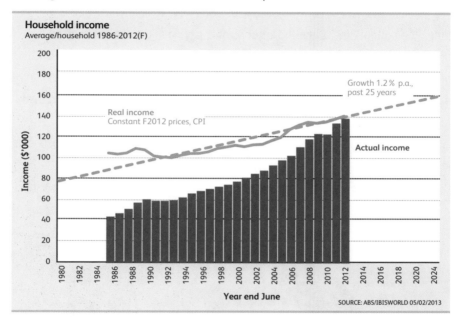

**Household income**
Average/household 1986-2012(F)

Real income
Constant F2012 prices, CPI

Growth 1.2% p.a., past 25 years

Actual income

Income ($'000)

Year end June

SOURCE: ABS/IBISWORLD 05/02/2013

Our 9 million households had an average gross income of $139,200 in 2012. It should be noted that some 8.5% of the income is an imputed (non-cash) contribution from home ownership, where owner-occupiers are assumed by statisticians to be landlords earning a rent (from themselves). Even without such imputation the average income is over $127,000 per household.

On average there are 1.3 workers per household, although the reality is that there are over one million homes without employees (but having incomes from investments, welfare or other sources). Such households include retirees, unemployed families and individuals (including students), and other welfare-dependent households.

On the present trajectory, the average income will pass a quarter of a million dollars by 2030. Of course, Australia has a polarisation of incomes as we well know. The richest 20% of households have 47% of the nation's gross household income, and the bottom 40% just 14%. As unfortunate as that is, there are three ameliorating factors.

First, the richest 20% of households don't have a net income that is 11 times the bottom 20%, since the latter quintile pay no taxes and get cash and non-cash benefits, rightly denied the rich and well-off; the ratio is nearer to 6:1 or less. Second, compared with the United States' polarisation we are almost an egalitarian population, but not quite, just a lot better than some nations. And third, rarely do the poor or rich stay that way all their lives.

The next two charts show the type of assets across the nation's households in F2012, and how the mix has changed over recent decades.

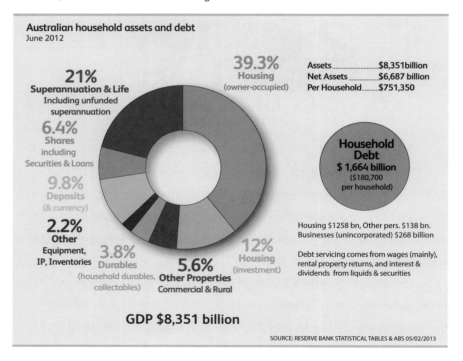

Australian household assets and debt
June 2012

39.3% Housing (owner-occupied)
21% Superannuation & Life Including unfunded superannuation
6.4% Shares including Securities & Loans
9.8% Deposits (& currency)
2.2% Other Equipment, IP, Inventories
3.8% Durables (household durables, collectables)
5.6% Other Properties Commercial & Rural
12% Housing (investment)

| Assets | $8,351billion |
| Net Assets | $6,687 billion |
| Per Household | $751,350 |

Household Debt
$ 1,664 billion
($180,700 per household)

Housing $1258 bn, Other pers. $138 bn. Businesses (unincorporated) $268 billion

Debt servicing comes from wages (mainly), rental property returns, and interest & dividends from liquids & securities

GDP $8,351 billion

SOURCE: RESERVE BANK STATISTICAL TABLES & ABS 05/02/2013

Housing is slowly heading to be less than half the value of all assets, and the proportion in durables (cars, furniture, appliances, etc.) is shrinking even faster.

In their place is the growing importance of financial assets, which have climbed from 27.5% of the total in 1989 to 38.3% in 2012. Indeed, financial assets are likely to be more than half of all assets before the middle of this century. Our superannuation system is leading this surge.

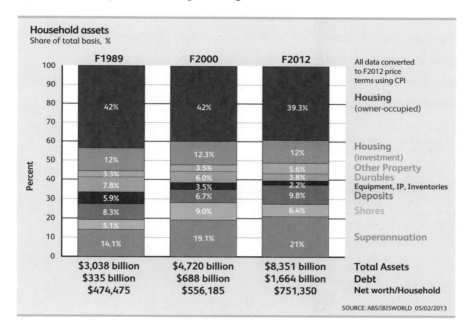

**Household assets**
Share of total basis, %

| | F1989 | F2000 | F2012 | |
|---|---|---|---|---|
| Housing (owner-occupied) | 42% | 42% | 39.3% | All data converted to F2012 price terms using CPI |
| Housing (investment) | 12% | 12.3% | 12% | |
| Other Property | 3.3% | 3.5% | 5.6% | |
| Durables | 7.8% | 6.0% | 3.8% | |
| Equipment, IP, Inventories | 5.9% | 3.5% | 2.2% | |
| Deposits | | 6.7% | 9.8% | |
| Shares | 8.3% | 9.0% | 6.4% | |
| | 5.1% | | | |
| Superannuation | 14.1% | 19.1% | 21% | |
| Total Assets | $3,038 billion | $4,720 billion | $8,351 billion | |
| Debt | $335 billion | $688 billion | $1,664 billion | |
| Net worth/Household | $474,475 | $556,185 | $751,350 | |

SOURCE: ABS/IBISWORLD 05/02/2013

Our average wealth (net worth) per household is climbing fast too, and the relative importance of assets is changing, as seen at the bottom of the third chart (above). In constant 2012 price terms, average net worth has risen from $474,475 in the late 1980s to just over $750,000 in 2012. We are expected to have millionaire households, in today's money terms, as the average sometime between 2025 and 2030.

Of course, we should not overlook debt. The debt proportion of total assets was 11% in 1989, but is now 20%. We would not want mortgage interest rates to go anywhere near the 15% of 1989 – two and a half times the current rate – as that would take the smile right off our faces. Then again, if most of our assets are financial – and therefore earning interest or dividends and capital gains – would it really matter? Indeed, financial assets now account for over half our net worth, given that the vast majority of the debt is housing related. But we cannot access our superannuation to pay our mortgage interest, so the servicing pain could be there with higher interest rates.

If the debt is taken off the appropriate assets in the pie chart above (i.e. mortgage debt off housing, and credit cards and loans off consumables), then we arrive at the net worth of households by type of asset. This is shown in the chart below, which highlights the even greater importance of financial assets (especially superannuation).

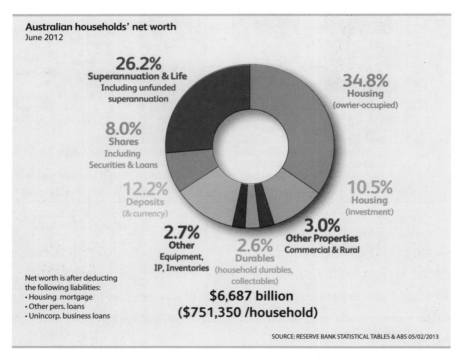

**Australian households' net worth**
June 2012

**26.2%**
**Superannuation & Life**
Including unfunded
superannuation

**8.0%**
**Shares**
Including
Securities & Loans

**12.2%**
Deposits
(& currency)

**2.7%**
**Other**
**Equipment,**
**IP, Inventories**

**2.6%**
Durables
(household durables,
collectables)

**3.0%**
**Other Properties**
**Commercial & Rural**

**34.8%**
**Housing**
(owner-occupied)

**10.5%**
**Housing**
(investment)

Net worth is after deducting
the following liabilities:
• Housing mortgage
• Other pers. loans
• Unincorp. business loans

**$6,687 billion**
**($751,350 /household)**

SOURCE: RESERVE BANK STATISTICAL TABLES & ABS 05/02/2013

Overall, we seem to be heading in a nice direction, and acting in a more financially literate way.